D1457382

You Can Cook

PAULA DUNAWAY SCHWARTZ

You Can Cook
HOW TO MAKE GOOD FOOD FOR YOUR FAMILY AND FRIENDS

Illustrated by Byron Barton

A Margaret K. McElderry Book / ATHENEUM NEW YORK 1976

For John and Matthew, who
cooked and tasted

My special thanks go to Carolyn Faria, for her
cookie recipe, and to Marian Vaillant, for her
coffeecake recipe. I am especially grateful to my
sons, Matthew and John, who gave me so much help
in testing the recipes.

Library of Congress Cataloging in Publication Data

Schwartz, Paula Dunaway.   You can cook.
"A Margaret K. McElderry book."
Summary: A cookbook for young people giving
step-by-step instructions for cooking meals for
people of all ages.   1. Cookery—Juvenile literature.
[1. Cookery]   I. Barton, Byron.   II. Title.
TX652.5.S35   641.5   76–12482
ISBN 0–689–50065–3

Designed by Suzanne Haldane

First Edition

Foreword

Young people are cooking more than ever before; cooking for fun, cooking to raise money for class trips or school equipment, cooking for school fairs, and cooking because often both parents work and must rely more on their children to pitch in and help. Young people want to become self-sufficient; they like to be counted on for help; they enjoy making things; and they enjoy good, ungimmicky food.

Cooking is fun because it appeals to the senses: you can touch what you cook, see it, taste it, and smell it. Also, cooking for someone else is a friendly thing. It is one way that you can express yourself to others—your friends and your families. To cook good food and share it is a special pleasure that everyone should have a chance to enjoy.

The recipes in this book have been chosen because they are simple but not unsophisticated. Any one of them could be served proudly to guests of any age. They are for "real" food —fresh food, cooked simply and with care. There are almost no canned or frozen ingredients included, because convenience foods do not taste nearly as good as fresh foods. Suggestions are made as to what may be served with the main courses to make a meal, and some sample menus are included. Preparation and cooking times are given for every recipe. If the meal consists of several parts, steps are indicated in their proper order. A number of dishes can be cooked ahead of time, and this is indicated in the recipes.

This book does not attempt to cover every kind of dish. From the simple recipes in this book you can move on to some of the many excellent books available for more experienced cooks.

It is assumed that anyone using this book will have done some cooking before, or, if not, will have some supervision, so the very elementary instructions are not included, such as basic cooking equipment, how to light the stove, how to peel and chop, and so on. It is also assumed that the young cook will be working in a kitchen that is already equipped, so the list of suggested equipment is very brief.

The food in this book is sturdy, filling, good-tasting, and not hard to make. It is for people of all ages, sizes, and tastes to share and for young people to cook.

Contents

A Few Basic Rules and Suggestions

Read all recipes through carefully and make sure you have everything you need before you start to cook. Plan your cooking time so that things will be ready at the same time. Cook whatever you can ahead of time. If you are planning a whole meal, don't do more than one complicated dish.

Always wash your hands before you start.

Don't ever be afraid to put your hands in the food while you are cooking or to get a bit messy. You can always wash up later.

Taste everything as you go along, and just before you are ready to serve it.

Season your food carefully. Too little is always better than too much. More seasoning can be added later if it is needed.

Serve hot food *hot,* unless it's something that actually tastes good warm, like fruit pies, baked apples, brown Betty, or baked ham, which is good at any temperature.

Serve food neatly and attractively—it makes a difference in how it tastes. Sprigs of parsley or chopped parsley make almost everything look better.

Follow the recipe exactly the first time or two you use it and then experiment if you want to. Don't be too upset if you make a mistake in measuring or timing; it's usually not too serious, and it is one way of learning.

Do not overcook vegetables. They become mushy.

Cook stews slowly, over low to medium heat. The meat will be more tender.

Always preheat the oven or broiler for 15 minutes.

Watch *very carefully* whatever you cook under the broiler, to make sure it doesn't burn; and be careful not to burn yourself.

Most meat should be at room temperature when you cook it (flank steak is one of the few exceptions) . This means taking it out of the refrigerator at least half an hour before you are ready to cook. Most fruits and vegetables also taste better if they are not too cold. Cold tends to kill flavor.

If you are the person who will be buying the groceries for what you cook, don't be afraid to ask the butcher questions, or even to ask him to do special things for you. This may be fun as you branch out in your cooking. Even in a supermarket, there is a butcher cutting up the meat, and usually you can ring a bell and ask him for what you want. A good butcher will be pleased by your interest and will give you what you ask for. You can learn a lot about meat this way.

Allow ½ pound of meat for each person, *if there is no bone*. For meat with bone, such as lamb shoulder for stew, or poultry, allow ¾ pound to 1 pound. Very bony meat, such as spareribs, requires even a little more than that. If in doubt, ask the butcher.

Cook over medium heat unless the recipe states otherwise. High heat is rarely necessary; when it is, the recipe will always say so.

Don't forget to stir things cooking on top of the stove often so they won't stick to the bottom of the pan.

"Cooking oil" in a recipe can be corn oil, olive oil, liquid Crisco, or any other of the oils found in supermarkets.

Safflower oil is especially good, as it is light and has relatively little taste or smell so that it can be used in salad dressings too.

Many families prefer using margarine to butter these days. Most of the recipes here can be cooked with either one. There are some recipes that call specifically for butter, because it is an important part of the taste. This is always clearly stated.

When you are cooking something in butter or margarine, the addition of a little oil to the pan will help to keep the fat from burning.

When rinsing out a hot skillet or frying pan, always use hot water, not cold.

Don't pour melted fat down the drain (butter, margarine, meat fat, bacon or sausage grease). Keep an empty coffee tin, or something with a plastic lid (not a glass jar: it may crack), and pour the fat into that before you wash out the pan. Cooking oil, however, can be washed down the drain with hot water.

Always keep several good thick potholders handy near the stove, and don't forget to use them. Never use a dishtowel instead of a potholder; it won't work.

Wear a large apron when you bake to keep the flour off your clothes. It's a good idea to wear one when you're cooking anything.

Leeks, parsley and spinach may be very sandy and should be rinsed carefully several times. Split leeks almost to the root with a knife and rinse down inside each layer. All salad greens should also be carefully washed, except for iceberg lettuce (the crunchy kind) which only needs a quick rinsing.

All baking powder called for in these recipes is double-acting; this is the kind found in most stores, and it will say so on the can. Single-acting requires double the amount called for in these recipes.

Fresh food always tastes better than frozen or canned, but there are some cases where a prepared food is so convenient and its taste is close enough to the fresh product that it is recommended. Some of the products on the market that are worth using if you must save time are: canned bouillon or bouillon cubes instead of homemade broth; frozen pie crusts; canned or frozen peas (they *must* be very small and tender), such as those put out by LeSueur; canned beets; canned gravy; mayonnaise (Hellmann's is one of the best).

Aluminum foil broiler pans are another commercial product that is a great convenience. They are not cheap, but it is wonderful to throw away a sticky broiler pan once in a while.

A few drops of lemon juice or vinegar added to stews, soups, all cooked dried beans, all cooked green vegetables and many others (stewed tomatoes, for instance) at the last minute sharpen the taste of the dish in a very nice way.

Some Measurements and Definitions

3 teaspoons equal 1 tablespoon
4 tablespoons equal ¼ cup
1 cup equals ½ pint
2 cups equal 1 pint
4 cups equal 2 pints or 1 quart
4 quarts equal 1 gallon

1 stick of butter or margarine equals 8 tablespoons
½ stick equals 4 tablespoons
¼ stick equals 2 tablespoons

If in doubt, divide the stick into eight
equal slices. Each slice will be a tablespoon.

1 stick of butter or margarine equals ½ cup melted
½ stick makes ¼ cup melted
2 sticks make 1 cup melted

Any kind of macaroni, spaghetti, or noodles doubles in volume when it is cooked. 2 cups of dried macaroni, for instance, will make 4 cups of cooked macaroni. So count on about ½ cup per person, dried. Be sure to boil it in plenty of water.

The thinner the spaghetti is, the more you will get when you cook it. Vermicelli, for instance, the thinnest kind of spaghetti, makes more than regular spaghetti. As a general rule, though, one pound box of spaghetti will make four average servings.

Rice triples in volume when it is cooked. 1 cup of dried rice makes 3 cups, cooked. Be sure to cook it in a big enough pot or it will boil over as it swells.

To *puree* something, such as a vegetable or a fruit, is to strain, crush, mash, blend, or put it through a food mill until it is a smooth mixture, like mashed potatoes.

To *baste* something means to spoon or pour small amounts of liquid over food as it is cooking. The liquid is usually the fat or juices in the pan, but may be anything—water and oil, wine, fruit juices, and so on. Perfect fried eggs, for instance, are made by basting the eggs with small spoonfuls of the butter or fat in which they are frying.

To *marinate* something is to let it stand in a seasoned liquid for a length of time before cooking it, so that it picks up the taste of the liquid, which is called the marinade. The marinade for lemon-broiled chicken, for example, consists of lemon juice, oil, salt, pepper, thyme, and onions (and garlic if you like it) .

To *separate eggs,* break the shell neatly and pour the yolk gently back and forth from one half shell to the other a few times, pouring out the white from the other shell into a bowl. Put the yolk into a separate bowl.

To *fold,* use a large metal or wooden spoon or a rubber spatula. Move it down through the mixture on the side farthest from you, then keep moving it toward you along the bottom of the dish and bring it up on the side near you. Folding is a way of mixing beaten egg whites or whipped cream with other ingredients so that the air stays in them.

It is a folding motion, bringing the heavier ingredients up from the bottom and tucking the lighter one down into it.

To *skim off fat,* tilt the pan so that the fat and meat juices run to one end. The fat is the clear liquid that is floating on top of the juice. Spoon this off into a container.

There are a few items which you may want to get if you don't have them and really enjoy cooking:

A *garlic press* is an easy way to crush garlic without getting it all over your hands. It has two handles and a little strainer-like compartment that you put the peeled garlic into; the handles press together to crush the garlic. It is inexpensive and can be found at any hardware store.

A *pepper mill* is a good thing to have. Freshly ground pepper tastes so much better than ground pepper that once you get used to its taste you will want to use it in almost any recipe that calls for pepper.

A *meat thermometer* is not essential, but it can be a great convenience, especially for an inexperienced cook. Be sure to get a good one, though. It will not be cheap, but it is worth the money. Follow the simple instructions that come with it, and don't put it in the dishwasher. It will tell you exactly when your roast is done. The only other way to find out is to cut into the meat with a knife and see for yourself.

A *rubber spatula* (the more you have the better) is good for many things. It is perfect for scraping the last drop out of bowls and pans, for stirring, for folding in egg whites without collapsing them, for turning things, and for making omelets.

Several pyrex (heat-proof glass) measuring cups in different sizes are helpful; one, two, and four-cup sizes are very useful.

A *vegetable peeler* is essential. Teach yourself to use it, if you don't know how, following the instructions that come with it, and it will save you a lot of time and trouble. It is inexpensive and available at any hardware store.

You Can Cook

VEGETABLE SOUP

Deciding just what vegetables to put in this soup, and all the peeling and chopping, can be fun. Just a few changes make a different soup, so do some experimenting each time you make this.

Serves: 4–6

Preparation time: about 30 minutes; heat the broth while you chop the vegetables (bouillon cubes and water can be used).

Cooking time: 30 minutes

What you will need:

> 6 cups broth (canned, homemade, or 6 cups
>   water and 6 bouillon cubes)
> 2 medium potatoes, peeled and chopped
> 1 medium onion, chopped
> ½ cup elbow macaroni or other small pasta
> 3 carrots, peeled and thinly sliced
> 2 stalks celery, chopped
> 1 cup canned tomatoes and liquid
> ½ cup raw string beans, cut in ½ inch pieces
> 1 small can red kidney beans (about 1 cup),
>   drained
> 1 small can of tiny peas *or* ½ package frozen
>   peas
> ⅓ cup chopped parsley, well rinsed
> salt and pepper
> grated Parmesan cheese

Add if you like:

¼ head of cabbage, shredded
1 turnip, peeled and sliced

a large pot, 3–4 quart size

How to cook it:

1. Bring the broth to a boil in the pot.

2. While the broth is heating, prepare the vegetables. When the broth boils, add the potatoes, carrots, celery, onion, green beans, tomatoes (and the cabbage and/or turnip, if you use them). Cook for 20 minutes.

3. Then add the macaroni, kidney beans, and peas and cook for 15 minutes more.

4. Taste for seasoning, and add salt and pepper to your taste. Add the chopped parsley.

Serving suggestion: Serve with lots of grated Parmesan cheese sprinkled in and plenty of good bread on the side.

SPLIT PEA SOUP

This soup can also be made with dried red or white beans, lentils, or black beans. It is a good idea to plan to make it after a baked ham dinner, so that you can use the ham bone and bits of leftover ham. Otherwise, buy a small piece of ham or ham hock instead. This is very good the day after it is made, as well.

Serves: 4–6

Planning your time: The peas must be soaked in cold water for several hours or overnight. Cooking time is 3 to 4 hours over low heat, until the peas are soft, but it doesn't need much attention once it is cooking.

What you will need:

1½ cups dried split peas
1 ham bone, piece of ham cut up, or ham hock
1 onion, peeled
1 stalk celery
1 bay leaf (if you have it)
8 cups water
salt and pepper
4 to 5 frankfurters

a large pot, 3–4 quart size

How to cook it:

1. Cover the peas with cold water and soak for several hours or overnight. Then drain them.

2. Put the peas, the ham bone, celery stalk, onion, bay leaf, and 8 cups of water into the pot. Bring it all to a boil, then

turn the heat down and simmer until the peas are soft and can be mashed easily with a fork. This will take about 2–3 hours. Stir it once in a while to make sure it doesn't stick.

3. When the peas are soft, take out the onion, celery, ham bone and bay leaf. Put 2 cups of the peas and liquid into the blender, puree them and put them back into the pot. Cut the meat off the ham bone and put that back in the soup. (If you like a smooth soup, puree all of it in the blender, and leave out the bits of ham from the bone.) Add salt and pepper to taste. If soup is too thick, add cream or milk.

4. In a separate pot, boil 4 or 5 hot dogs for 15 minutes. Cut them into chunks and add to the soup when you are ready to serve.

Serving suggestion: This soup is very filling and makes a good meal, with salad, bread, and dessert.

BLENDER SOUPS

These are creamy vegetable soups, and they can be delicious hot or cold. You can make many different kinds, according to the vegetables you use. They are fast and easy to prepare and are a fine beginning to any meal. If served with sandwiches, they make a delicious lunch. This kind of soup can be made ahead and is very good the next day. In the summertime, it is good cold. If you do not have a blender, you can put the vegetables through a Foley Food Mill, which you turn by hand. It's inexpensive and available in any hardware store.

Serves: 4

Preparation time: about 30 minutes to prepare the vegetables

Cooking time: about 30 minutes

What you will need:

2 cups chicken or beef broth (use canned or
   homemade broth, or 2 bouillon cubes and
   2 cups water)
1–2 tablespoons butter
1 small onion, peeled and chopped
2 stalks celery, cut up small
1 small potato, sliced
1 cup of any of the following vegetables: peas,
   lima beans, spinach (use 2 cups, washed and
   chopped), carrots (peeled and sliced),
   canned tomatoes, broccoli (only the tops,
   washed), cucumber (use 2 cups, peeled and
   chopped), cauliflower (washed and broken
   into small bunches). Frozen peas, lima beans
   or spinach are fine for this soup; defrost
   them first
1 cup cream or milk
salt and pepper

a 2-quart pot
a smaller pot for the broth

How to cook it:

1. Melt the butter in the larger pot over low heat. Begin heating the broth in the small pot.

2. Add the chopped onion and celery to the butter and cook for 5 minutes, until it looks slightly transparent.

3. Add the hot broth, the potato, and whatever vegetable you decide to use. When it comes to a boil, cook it gently for 20 minutes, or until all the vegetables are just cooked.

4. Put it all into the blender (you may have to do it in 2 or 3 steps. Don't fill blender more than ¾ full). Keep your hand on the lid and blend until smooth.

5. Pour the soup back into the pot, add the milk or cream (or half and half), and taste for seasoning. Add salt and pepper to your taste. When you are ready to serve it, heat it well but don't boil it.

Poultry

ROAST CHICKEN

Serves: 4

Preparation time: 5 minutes

Cooking time: 1½ hours

What you will need:

> 1 roasting chicken, about 3–4 pounds
> salt and pepper
> ½ teaspoon thyme
> cooking oil

> Add if you like:

> 4 medium potatoes, peeled and quartered
> 4 medium onions, peeled and quartered
> 6 carrots, peeled and halved
> parsley

> a roasting pan

How to cook it:

1. Preheat oven to 450°.

2. Take the giblets and neck out of the chicken.

3. Rub chicken all over with cooking oil and sprinkle with salt, pepper, and thyme. Put it in the roasting pan in the oven and turn heat down to 400°. Cook the chicken for 1½ hours, turning it once or twice, until it is brown and crisp on the outside. Pour a little oil mixed with water over it 2 or 3 times so it won't get too dry. If you want to roast potatoes with this, put them in the pan at the beginning along with a little extra oil or butter for them to brown in. You can also put in onions and carrots. If you do, make sure there is enough butter or oil in the pan so they don't dry out, and salt and pepper them at the end.

Serving suggestions: Serve all together on a platter garnished with parsley, and a dish of applesauce on the side.

For a special meal, serve a blender soup first, a green salad with the chicken, and a fruit pie or hot apple dessert.

FRIED CHICKEN

Serves: 6

Preparation time: 10 minutes

Cooking time: 45 minutes–1 hour

What you will need:

    2 frying chickens, 2⅓–3 pounds each, cut into
      serving pieces

1½ cups flour
salt and pepper
1½ teaspoons baking powder
1 cup milk
shortening or cooking oil
a large, heavy frying pan with a lid

How to cook it:

1. Put the flour, baking powder, 1 teaspoon salt, ¼ teaspoon pepper in a plastic bag.

2. Put the milk in a bowl. Dip the chicken pieces, one at a time in the milk, then shake them in the bag of flour, holding it tightly closed.

3. Heat shortening or oil in the frying pan until very hot. The oil or fat should be about 1 inch deep. Be careful not to let it splatter you when you put the chicken into it.

4. When the oil is hot, cook the chicken pieces in it over medium heat, turning to make sure they brown evenly on all sides, and watching carefully to prevent burning. There will probably not be room for all the pieces in one pan. Either use two pans, or brown the chicken a few pieces at a time, taking out the brown pieces as you go. When they are all brown, put them all into the pan (or pans) and cook covered for 30 minutes over medium flame, moving the pieces so they all cook evenly. Remove the lid for the last 10 minutes so the pieces will be crisp when you serve them. *Or,* you can preheat the oven to 450°, spread the browned pieces in a baking pan, dribble a little of the

cooking fat over them and cook in the oven for 45 minutes. They do not need to be turned.

Serving suggestion: Serve with mashed potatoes, green salad, and blueberry pie for dessert.

LEMON-BROILED CHICKEN

This has a delicious, slightly lemony taste. It is also very good cold.

Serves: 4–6

Preparation time: 20 minutes to make the marinade; the chicken should sit in it for at least an hour before you cook it —the longer the better.

Cooking time: 45 minutes–1 hour

What you will need:

2 small broiling chickens, cut in quarters
⅓ cup lemon juice
⅔ cup cooking oil
1 teaspoon salt
¼ teaspoon pepper

1 small onion, chopped
1 teaspoon thyme or tarragon (you can
    substitute 1 clove garlic, crushed, if you
    prefer)

a large bowl
a broiler pan

How to cook it:

1. Combine the lemon juice, oil, salt, pepper, onion, and thyme or tarragon. Put the chicken pieces in a large bowl and pour the mixture over them. Make sure every piece is covered with a little of the marinade mixture. Let it sit at room temperature for an hour or more before cooking. (Or prepare it in the morning and leave it in the refrigerator all day.)

2. Preheat broiler to 450°.

3. Spread the chicken pieces in the broiler pan and put under the broiler several inches from the flame. Look at it in 20 minutes, and baste it with a little of the lemon-oil mixture several times while it cooks. Turn the pieces to make sure they brown on both sides, ending with the skin side up. They should be crisp and brown. If they are not cooking fast enough, either move the pan closer to the flame or turn up the flame, but be sure to watch carefully so they do not burn.

Serving suggestion: This is good with rice and a salad. A fruit pie for dessert would make it a real company meal.

MUSTARD CHICKEN

Preparation time: If possible, an hour or two for the chicken to soak in the sauce; 15 minutes for the sauce and to preheat oven.

Serves: 8

Cooking time: about $1\frac{1}{2}$ hours

What you will need:

> 2 small broiling chickens, cut in quarters
> 1 small onion, peeled and chopped
> 1 clove garlic, peeled and cut in half
> 4 tablespoons vinegar (any kind)
> 1 teaspoon salt
> $\frac{1}{4}$ teaspoon pepper
> 4 tablespoons (12 teaspoons) brown mustard,
>   like Gulden's
> 2 tablespoons catsup
>
> a large roasting pan

How to cook it:

1. Mix together in a small bowl the onion, salt, pepper, vinegar, mustard, and catsup.

2. Put the chicken pieces in a roasting pan. Pour the vinegar-mustard mixture over them, and with your hands or a fork, make sure the pieces are covered with the sauce. Let them sit at room temperature for 1–2 hours if you can.

3. Preheat oven to 375°.

4. Put the roasting pan with the chicken in it into the oven and bake for 1½ hours, turning the chicken once or twice. It should be nicely browned. Cut into a thick piece to make sure it isn't pink. If necessary, raise the heat a little.

Serving suggestions: Serve on a platter; pour the pan juices over the chicken.

Serve with rice and a salad of sliced tomatoes, and with gingerbread for dessert.

ROAST DUCK

Preparation time: 5 minutes, but if you get a frozen duck, be sure to allow several hours for thawing; 15 minutes to preheat oven.

Serves: 4

Cooking time: 2 hours

What you will need:

   1 duck, 5–6 pounds
   salt and pepper

   Add if you like:

   4 medium potatoes, peeled and quartered
   1 large can of sauerkraut, rinsed and well drained

a roasting pan, about 2 inches deep

How to cook it:

1. Preheat oven to 450°.

2. Rinse the duck in cold water and dry it with paper towels. Sprinkle it inside and out with salt and pepper. Put it in the roasting pan, which should be about 2 inches deep to hold the duck fat as it runs off. Prick the duck in several places with a sharp fork to let the fat run off, and do this at least 3 or 4 times while it cooks. Turn it over after an hour, and then again after 40 minutes, so the top will be crisp and dark when you finish. There will be a lot of fat in the pan, and you should try to remove it once or twice while the duck cooks; be very careful doing this. A bulb baster is the easiest thing to use. Put the fat in an empty tin. Save 1/4 cup of the fat to cook sauerkraut in, if you are serving it with the duck.

3. If you are having roast potatoes, put them in the pan when you start the duck, and turn them once or twice. They will brown beautifully in the duck fat.

4. To cook the sauerkraut, pour 1/4 cup duck fat in a heavy pan, heat it, and add the drained sauerkraut. Cook over a low fire for an hour, stirring and turning once or twice. It is delicious with the duck.

Serving suggestion: Serve a bowl of cold applesauce with the duck. Try fresh fruit for dessert.

VARIATIONS ON PLAIN ROAST DUCK

Roast Duck Stuffed with Sauerkraut

Serves: 4

Preparation time: ¾ hour (including 15 minutes to pre-heat oven) to prepare the sauerkraut; do this ahead if you can, as it is easier to stuff the duck if the sauerkraut is not hot.

Cooking time: 2 hours

What you will need:

1 duck, 5–6 pounds
4 strips bacon
1 apple, peeled, cored, and chopped
1 onion, peeled and chopped
1 large can of sauerkraut

a heavy frying pan
a roasting pan, about 2 inches deep

How to cook it:

1. Fry the bacon over low heat until most of the fat is out of it. Remove it from the pan, let drain on paper towels and use for something else. Leave the fat in the pan.

2. Cook the chopped onion and apple over a low flame in the bacon fat for about 5 minutes. Add the sauerkraut and cook it, stirring, over a medium flame for about 15 minutes. Let it cool a little.

3. Prepare the duck according to instructions for plain roast duck (see p. 20). Then stuff the duck with the sauerkraut and roast according to instructions for plain roast duck.

Serving suggestion: Serve with mashed or pan-roasted potatoes and applesauce, and fresh fruit or lemon sherbet for dessert.

Pepper Duck

Serves: 4

Preparation time: 15 minutes, including time to preheat oven

Cooking time: 2 hours

What you will need:

   1 duck, 5–6 pounds
   3 tablespoons peppercorns

   a roasting pan, about 2 inches deep

How to cook it:

1. Put the peppercorns in the blender and whirl until they are crushed. Press the cracked pepper all over the duck. It will seem like a lot of pepper, but it will not be hot—the cooking somehow takes the bite out of the pepper and gives it an unusual and delicious taste.

2. Roast as for plain roast duck (see p. 20).

Serving suggestions: Sauerkraut is good with this, too. Or you could serve it with pan-roasted potatoes and a green salad. Fruit bowl would be a good dessert.

Roasts, Steaks, and Chops

PAN-BROILED STEAKS AND CHOPS

This is the best method for very good, juicy meat, like lamb chops (rib or loin) and porterhouse, sirloin, or shell steaks. They are all expensive. Cooking this way makes the kitchen quite smelly and smoky, but the taste is delicious and worth a little extra cleaning up. Do close the kitchen door, though, and open a window or turn on a fan if you have one.

Preparation time: none

Cooking time: 15–25 minutes, depending on how you like your meat

What you will need:

steaks or chops, 1 inch–1½ inches thick,
  allowing ½–¾ pounds per person (or one
  chop per person)
salt

a heavy frying pan

How to cook it:

1. Sprinkle salt over the bottom of the frying pan till the surface is lightly covered. Heat the skillet over high heat until it is very hot and the salt begins to turn brown and smoke a little.

2. Turn the heat down slightly, to medium-high. Put the meat in and brown it for 5 minutes on each side. Then lower the heat slightly, to medium, and continue to cook for almost ten minutes, turning the meat once or twice so that it cooks evenly.

3. With a sharp knife make a small, deep cut in the meat to check for doneness. Try not to let too much juice out. The meat will have a delicious brown crust on the outside and should be tender and juicy inside. Some people like it rare; some prefer it well done. Ask your guests or family ahead of time if you can. If necessary, you can cut a piece from the steak when it is rare, and serve that, leaving the other piece in the pan to cook a few minutes longer for the person who likes it well done.

Serving suggestion: Baked potato and a salad, and chocolate mousse for dessert would make a delicious meal.

ROAST BEEF

The best roasts are expensive: they are sirloin roast; rib roast with the bones in (it is called standing rib roast and it looks magnificent when served; allow 1 pound per person), boneless rib roast and rump.

Planning your time: Let the roast stand 1–3 hours at room temperature before you cook it, if you have the time; if not it can go directly from the refrigerator to the oven; 15 minutes to preheat oven.

Preparation time: none

Cooking time: 1½–2 hours

What you will need:

1 roast of beef, 3–5 pounds, depending on how
    many people it is for. Allow 1 pound per
    person for a standing rib roast. Leftover
    beef is delicious, so don't be afraid of having
    too much. Do not get a roast smaller than
    3 pounds if boneless, or 3 ribs if it is a
    standing rib roast
salt and pepper

Add if you like:

1 medium-sized potato, peeled and quartered,
  per person

a roasting pan

How to cook it:

1. Preheat oven to 450°.

2. Wipe the roast with a damp cloth or paper towel, and sprinkle with salt and pepper. Put it in the roasting pan and place in the oven.

3. If you like, put the potatoes in the pan when you start the meat. Salt them, and turn them once.

4. After 20–25 minutes, when the roast has begun to brown, turn the oven heat down to 375°. Cook for another hour, and then test for doneness (unless you are using a meat thermometer). If it is just a *little* rarer than you want it, turn the oven off and leave it in another 15 or 20 minutes. If it is done, take it out and let it sit on top of the stove for 10 minutes. It will slice better if you do.

5. When done, put the roast on a platter and put the potatoes, if any, around it or in a separate bowl.

6. Tilt the pan so the fat and meat juice run to one end of it. Then skim off the fat (the clear liquid floating on top of the juice) into a container to be discarded. Add ½ cup

of water to the pan, stir and scrape the bottom over a medium flame until the juice is hot and brown. Put in a pitcher or bowl and pass with the meat.

Serving suggestions: Serve with horseradish or mustard and green peas.

A meal with a roast deserves a special dessert—try beautiful strawberry pie or gingerbread with whipped cream.

MARINATED FLANK STEAK

As this has no bone, there is no waste. Allow about ½ pound per person, or a little more. A 2-pound steak will feed four. This is a long, flat, rather stringy-looking steak that is delicious and tender, but *must* be carved in thin, slanting slices, the short way across, against the grain of the meat, when it is served. The longer the meat marinates, the better.

Serves: 4

Planning your time: 1–4 hours to soak the meat in the marinade before cooking; includes 15 minutes to preheat oven.

Preparation time: 10 minutes for the marinade; 1–4 hours ahead for marinating

Cooking time: 20–30 minutes for broiling the meat

What you will need:

½ cup soy sauce, preferably imported
   (Kikkoman is a good brand)
¾ cup red wine, if you can get it, or ¼ cup
   vinegar mixed with ½ cup water
1 clove garlic, peeled and cut in half
1 flank steak, 2 pounds or more

a shallow dish
a broiler pan

How to cook it:

1. Rub the cut garlic all over the meat; then throw it out. Put the meat in a shallow dish or pan. Combine soy sauce and wine and pour them over the meat. Put in the refrigerator for at least an hour, and turn the meat over once while it is soaking.

2. Preheat broiler (highest heat) for 15 minutes.

3. Take the steak out of the marinade and put it in a broiler pan under the broiler, fairly close to the flame. Cook about ten minutes on each side, pouring the wine–soy sauce mixture over it a little at a time. Check with a knife for doneness. Put the meat on a platter. Pour the wine–soy sauce mixture from the broiling pan into a pitcher and serve with meat. If it seems to have dried up, just pour some very hot water (about ½ cup) into the pan, scrape the bottom and stir the brown bits into it. Then pour this into a pitcher and serve with meat.

Note: *Remember to cut the meat in thin, cross-grain, diagonal slices.*

Serving suggestions: This is especially good with baked or mashed potatoes and a salad of green beans or sliced tomatoes and onions.

Use leftovers with rice.

ROAST LEG OF LAMB

Planning your time: If you have the time, take the roast out of the refrigerator an hour before you are ready to put it in to cook; if not, put it directly into the oven from the refrigerator.

Serves: 6

Preparation time: 15 minutes to preheat oven; 20–30 minutes if you add vegetables to the pan

Cooking time: 2 hours for well-done lamb; 1½ hours for pink lamb

What you will need:

1 leg of lamb, 5–6 pounds
1–2 tablespoons flour

salt and pepper
½ teaspoon thyme
1 garlic clove, peeled and cut in half (optional)

Add if you like:

6 medium potatoes, peeled and quartered
6–8 carrots, peeled and halved
6–8 small onions, peeled

a roasting pan

How to cook it:

1. Preheat oven to 375°.

2. Wipe the meat with a damp cloth or paper towel. If you like garlic with lamb, as many people do, rub the roast all over with the cut garlic clove. Then throw the garlic out. Rub the meat all over with flour. Sprinkle with salt and pepper and the thyme.

3. Put the lamb in the oven and roast without basting for about 2 hours (about 1½ hours if you like it pink). Cut into it to check for doneness.

4. If you like, add any or all of the vegetables mentioned. Put them in at the beginning, and turn and baste them once or twice with the pan juice or a little water.

5. When done, put the lamb on a platter and put the vegetables, if any, around it or in a separate bowl.

6. Tilt the pan so the fat and meat juice run to one end of it. Then skim off the fat (the clear liquid floating on top of the juice) into a container to be discarded. Add ½ cup of water to the pan, stir and scrape the bottom over a medium flame until the juice is hot and brown. Put in a pitcher or bowl and pass with the meat.

Serving suggestions: Another vegetable good with lamb is tomato—either as a salad, or cut in half, seasoned with salt and pepper, and baked in the oven for 30 minutes, while the lamb is roasting.

Cold sliced lamb is good served with mustard, pickles, good bread, and a salad.

You can also use it in shepherd's pie or a meat salad.

ROAST LEG OF LAMB WITH MUSTARD

This may sound strange, but it is juicy, delicious, and not too spicy. It is very good with dried white beans, cooked according to the recipe for split pea soup, but use 2 cups less water and don't let them get mushy, and don't puree them. Stir in a small can of tomatoes if you like. Or use canned white beans; heat them well and season with salt and pepper and a good chunk of butter. Add some pan juice too.

Preparation time: 15 minutes; take the meat out of the refrigerator an hour before cooking if you have time; if not it can go directly into the oven

Cooking time: 2 hours

What you will need:

1 leg of lamb, 5–6 pounds
½ cup brown mustard, such as Gulden's (yellow
   will *not* do)
2 tablespoons cooking oil
1 teaspoon thyme
1 clove garlic, peeled and mashed
2 tablespoons soy sauce

a roasting pan

How to cook it:

1. Mix the mustard, oil, soy sauce, garlic and thyme together
   very well. Spread this mixture all over the leg of lamb, using a brush, rubber spatula, or the back of a spoon. If you
   have time, let it sit at room temperature for an hour before
   you cook it, to pick up the flavor.

2. Preheat the oven to 375°.

3. Put the lamb in a roasting pan and cook without basting
   for two hours (less if you like it a bit pink). If the mustard smells as if it's burning, add a little water to the pan
   from time to time.

4. Remove the roast when it is done and put it on a platter.
   Pour ½ cup water into the pan, scrape the bottom and stir
   it over a medium flame for a minute; serve this pan juice
   in a pitcher with the meat.

Serving suggestions: This is good with white beans and tomatoes, and watercress or green salad. It is also good with roast, baked, or mashed potatoes, and green beans or salad. Baked tomatoes go well with it, too, or carrots, peas, or lima beans.

Leftover lamb is delicious sliced and served cold with mustard, pickles, good bread, and a salad. You can also use it in shepherd's pie or a meat salad.

BAKED HAM

This is a good and very easy meal if you have to feed a large number of people, and if there is ham left over, it is delicious cold or cooked for breakfast with eggs. Also, it will keep for several days. Plan to make split pea soup or one of the bean dishes afterwards, and use the ham bone, or a chunk of the ham if it is boneless. A good ham is not cheap, but it goes a long way. A 6-pound boneless ham will serve 10–12 people. An 8-pound ham with bone in will serve 6–8.

Planning your time: Most hams sold in supermarkets do not need long cooking. They can be bought with a bone or without; either way, plan on $1\frac{1}{2}$ hours cooking time at most. The ham can be cooked and ready an hour before you eat, and it can be served lukewarm or at room temperature, as well as hot, which makes it a good choice for a large party.

Preparation time: 15 minutes for glazing the ham and pre-heating the oven

Cooking time: 1 hour or a little longer

What you will need:

1 ham (allow ½ pound per person; if the bone
  is very large, allow ¾ pound)
1 cup brown sugar
2 teaspoons dry mustard
cloves
a little orange juice or any liquid (any other
  fruit juice or any soft drink will do)

a roasting pan

How to cook it:

1. Preheat oven to 350°.

2. Cut the brown rind, if there is one, off the top of the whole ham, using a sharp knife and pulling away the rind as you cut it. Leave a layer of fat on the ham. With a sharp knife, cut a diamond pattern all over the top of the fat. Stick cloves at the corners of the diamonds. Mix the mustard and brown sugar together and add just enough liquid to make a thick paste (1–2 tablespoons should be plenty). Then spread the brown sugar and mustard mixture over the top of the ham, put it in the roasting pan and bake it at 350° for 1 hour and 15 minutes.

Serving suggestions: Serve hot or warm with buttered green noodles and a tomato salad, or cold with coleslaw or potato salad and perhaps apple pie for dessert.

GLAZING SAUCE FOR PORK

This is an easy barbecue sauce which is delicious on roast pork, spareribs, or pork chops, either oven-baked or broiled. It can also be brushed on roast duck. It makes a delicious dark brown crust on the meat. Any leftover sauce will keep for weeks in a jar in the refrigerator.

Preparation time: 10 minutes

What you will need:

½ cup soy sauce
½ cup catsup
¼ cup honey
1 clove garlic

How to cook it:

1. Peel outer skin off the garlic and mash it with a garlic press, the back of a big spoon, or even a hammer.

2. Mix together the soy sauce, catsup, honey, and crushed garlic.

3. Brush on the meat several times while cooking. Use pastry brush, rubber spatula or the back of a spoon.

ROAST PORK

Pork takes long, slow cooking, and must never be pink, which means it is not thoroughly cooked. It must always be well done. Of the pork roasts, the loin center cut is the best (and most expensive) . The next best is the loin end. The rib end will have the most bones and the least meat. Whatever cut you choose, ask the butcher to crack the bone between each chop so that the roast can be easily sliced.

Serves: 6

Preparation time: none, except 15 minutes to preheat oven

Cooking time: 2 to 2½ hours for a 6-pound roast

What you will need:

  1 6-pound roast of pork (allow 1 pound per
    person, or 2 chops each)
  salt and pepper
  thyme

Add if you like:

6 potatoes, peeled and cut in quarters
6 small onions, peeled and cut in half
1 1-pound can sauerkraut, rinsed in cold water
   and drained in a sieve so that it is as dry as
   possible

a large roasting pan

How to cook it:

1. Preheat the oven to 350°.

2. Wipe the roast with a damp cloth and rub it with salt, pepper, and thyme. Put it in the roasting pan and cook for two hours. Test for doneness by cutting deep into the roast with a sharp knife. If still pink, raise the heat to 375° and cook another half hour.

3. If you want to cook onions and sauerkraut with the meat, put them in one end of the pan when you put the meat in the oven. Turn with a fork a few times while they are cooking.

4. If you decide to cook potatoes with the meat, put them in after 45 minutes. Turn them once or twice so that they will brown on all sides.

Variation: Brush the roast with glazing sauce and cook according to directions above. Brush once or twice with more sauce while it is cooking.

Serving suggestion: Serve with applesauce and a green salad. Peach pie would be good for dessert.

PORK CHOPS

Pork chops may be broiled or baked in the oven. Broiling is quicker, but it tends to dry the meat out. If you use this method, thin chops are best, as they do not have to cook for so long. For thick chops, a slow baking in the oven will give better results. Remember that pork must be thoroughly cooked and never pink inside.

Preparation time: 15 minutes for preheating oven and making sauce

Cooking time: *For broiling,* about 30 minutes, for thin chops and about 50 minutes for chops one inch thick.
   For baking, about an hour for thin chops and about an hour and a half for chops one inch thick.

What you will need:

   1 large or 2 small pork chops per person
   glazing sauce (see p. 35)

   a roasting pan or broiler pan

How to cook it:

For broiling

1. Preheat oven to 450°.

2. With a pastry brush or rubber spatula or the back of a spoon, brush the chops with glazing sauce and put under the broiler 2 or 3 inches from the flame. Brush several more times with sauce while cooking and turn 2 or 3 times until the chops are dark brown and well done.

For baking

1. Preheat oven to 375°.

2. Brush the chops with glazing sauce, using a pastry brush or a rubber spatula or the back of a spoon. Put them in the oven and brush them several more times with sauce while baking. Be sure to turn them over at least once during the baking.

Whether broiling or baking, cut into chops with a sharp knife to make sure they are no longer pink. Cooking time will vary according to thickness.

Serving suggestions: Serve with applesauce, baked or mashed potatoes, and green salad or cole slaw. Blueberry pie would be good for dessert.

SPARERIBS

Spareribs have a lot of fat on them, so they need a long cooking time to let it melt away. They are also bony, so you must allow a pound (or even a little more) for each person. They should be dark and crisp when done.

Planning your time: Allow an hour and a quarter to an hour and a half. If you put potatoes in the oven to bake while the spareribs are broiling under a medium flame, they will be ready at about the same time. Wrap them in foil so the high heat will not harden the skins.

Preparation time: 15–20 minutes for the sauce and for preheating the oven

Cooking time: 1 hour and 15 minutes

What you will need:

>   4–5 pounds spareribs
>   glazing sauce (see p. 35)
>   salt and pepper
>
>   a large broiler pan

How to cook it:

1. Preheat broiler to 400°.

2. Wipe the spareribs with a damp cloth or paper towel, and sprinkle them with salt and pepper. Cut them into sections

of four ribs each and put them in the broiler pan. Spread the glazing sauce over the ribs and put the pan under the broiler flame, 2–3 inches from the heat.

3. Put more sauce on them in about 20 minutes, and when they are brown, turn them with a long fork and do the same with the other side. Turn them again 10 minutes before you take them out.

Spareribs can also be cooked in the oven. Follow the same procedure, but use the oven heat instead of the broiler heat. Turn it to 450° and allow an extra 15 minutes cooking time.

Serving suggestion: Serve with mashed potatoes, sauerkraut, and a salad—and lots of paper napkins. Baked apples with cream would be good for dessert.

Casseroles and Stews

BASIC TOMATO SAUCE
for Spaghetti, Lasagne, or Macaroni

Make this ahead and reheat it. It is good for 2 or 3 days. Or make a lot of it and freeze what you don't use. (To freeze, let sauce cool, then pour into plastic containers or glass jars with tight-fitting lids, and store in freezer. Do not fill containers all the way up, as sauce will expand with the cold and the glass may break.)

Serves: 4

Preparation time: 10 minutes

Cooking time: 20–30 minutes

What you will need:

> 1 large can of tomatoes (35-ounce size)
> 1 small onion, chopped very fine
> 1 clove garlic, peeled and cut in half
> 2 tablespoons butter or oil
> ½ teaspoon salt
> ¼ teaspoon pepper

Add if you like:

> ½ teaspoon oregano
> ½ teaspoon basil
> 2 tablespoons tomato paste, if you want to
>   thicken the sauce

> a medium-sized saucepan, 1–2 quart size

How to cook it:

1. Heat the butter or oil in the saucepan and add the onion and garlic. Cook it for 5–10 minutes over a low flame, until it looks pale yellow and transparent. Remove the garlic.

2. Add the can of tomatoes, and crush them as they cook, using a spoon and a fork. Add the tomato paste, if the sauce does not seem thick enough.

3. Add salt and pepper to your taste (try ½ teaspoon salt and ¼ teaspoon pepper). Add oregano and/or basil, if you like. Cook over low flame for 20–30 minutes, uncovered.

Note: Double this recipe for lasagne (see p. 46).

SPAGHETTI AND MEATBALLS

Serves: 4

Planning your time:

1. Make sauce (see p. 41).

2. Boil spaghetti water.

3. Mix meatballs and cook them.

4. 5–10 minutes after you start cooking the meatballs, put the spaghetti into the boiling water.

5. Heat up the sauce on a low flame.

Spaghetti

This recipe is good for any pasta: noodles, macaroni, and such.

Preparation time: 20 minutes to boil the water

Cooking time: 10 minutes

What you will need:

    1 pound box of spaghetti (any kind will do)
    1 teaspoon salt
    1 tablespoon oil
    butter or margarine
    grated cheese

    a large pot, 8-quart size
    a large strainer or colander

How to cook it:

1. Fill the pot nearly full with water (about 6 quarts); bring it to a boil. Add 1 tablespoon salt and 1 tablespoon oil.

2. When the water is boiling hard, add the spaghetti to it. Push the ends in gently with a big spoon till they are all in, and stir with a long fork to make sure they don't stick together.

3. After the spaghetti has cooked for 7 minutes, pull out a strand with a fork and taste it. It should be a little chewy but not at all hard. Keep testing until it's done. It will take 8–10 minutes.

4. When it is done, pour the spaghetti into a colander or large strainer, drain it, then put it into a bowl with a large chunk of butter or margarine. Mix well and serve with meatballs, sauce, and grated cheese.

Meatballs

Preparation time: 5 minutes

Cooking time: 15–20 minutes

What you will need:

1½ pounds ground beef
3 tablespoons grated cheese
2 eggs
3 slices of bread (white or whole wheat)
1 teaspoon salt
¼ teaspoon pepper or less
a pinch of garlic salt
3 tablespoons cooking oil

a large, heavy frying pan

How to cook it:

1. Put meat, eggs, cheese, pepper, and salt into a bowl. Add a pinch of garlic salt.

2. Wet the 3 slices of bread in cold water and squeeze them in both hands to get the water out. They will get soft and sticky. Hold them over the bowl and crumble the bread as small as you can. Mix everything together very well with a fork.

3. Pour 3 tablespoons of oil into a big frying pan and heat it over a medium flame.

4. Shape meatballs about the size of walnuts and put them in the hot oil. Don't crowd them too close together.

5. Keep turning them with a spoon until they are brown and crisp on all sides. Take them out and put them on a piece of paper towel to drain the oil off. Put more in if you haven't used all the meat mixture yet. If the meatballs are done before the spaghetti, put them in an oven-proof dish or pan, turn the oven to 250°, and keep them warm in the oven until you are ready.

Serving suggestions: You can serve the meatballs in a separate bowl from the spaghetti, or put the spaghetti on a big platter with the meatballs all around it. If you plan to have sauce, serve it on the side, in a bowl or pitcher. Serve plenty of grated cheese also.

Serve this with a green salad and for dessert have fresh fruit and cookies.

LASAGNE

This can be put together several hours ahead of time and cooked just before you are ready to serve it; or it can be put together and frozen, then thawed and cooked when you want it. Follow directions below, but instead of baking, wrap the dish in foil and store in freezer. This recipe serves 6 generously.

Serves: 6

Planning your time: If you use homemade sauce, make it ahead. It will take about 40 minutes. Once you have boiled the lasagne, all you have to do is put the ingredients together and bake.

Preparation time: about 45 minutes, including 15 minutes to preheat oven

Cooking time: 45 minutes

What you will need:

1 package lasagne
3 tablespoons cooking oil
1 tablespoon salt
¾ pound ground beef (about what you would use for 3 good-sized hamburgers)
4–5 cups tomato sauce canned (2 16-ounce cans or jars) or homemade (double the recipe on p. 41)
1 pound ricotta or cottage cheese
1 pound mozarella cheese, sliced (don't worry if it crumbles into bits)
1 cup grated Parmesan cheese (or more if you like it). Buy the kind that is already grated

a rectangular baking dish, about 2 inches deep, 14 inches long, and 9 inches wide
a medium-sized pot for the sauce (at least 6-cup size)
a large pot for the lasagne (should hold 1½ gallons)
a colander

How to cook it:

1. If you are going to bake the lasagne right away, preheat the oven to 350°.

2. Brown the meat in the pot with 1 tablespoon cooking oil. Then pour off the extra oil or fat, leaving the meat in, add the sauce, and heat for 20 minutes over medium heat.

3. Fill the large pot with water, add 1 tablespoon salt, 2 tablespoons cooking oil, and bring to a boil. When the water is boiling, add the lasagne, and boil for 8–10 minutes or until just tender. Keep stirring the lasagne with a long fork so they will not stick together.

4. While the lasagne and the sauce are cooking, set out the baking dish, ricotta, mozarella, and grated cheese.

5. When the lasagne is done (it should be tender but still chewy, like spaghetti), drain it into a large colander, run cold water over it for a minute or two, and bring it over to your worktable. Work as quickly as you can so the lasagne won't get too sticky, but don't worry if the strips do stick and tear. It won't show when you're done.

6. Spread ½ cup sauce on the bottom of the baking dish. Then put a layer of lasagne over it (3 or 4 strips). Put spoonfuls of ricotta or cottage cheese, bits of mozarella, and a sprinkling of grated cheese on the lasagne. Then pour about ½ cup sauce over it. Then do another layer of lasagne, a layer of the 3 cheeses, and the sauce again. If you

have enough left over, do another layer, ending with the sauce on top. All the cheese and sauce should be used up when you finish.

7. Bake the lasagne for 45 minutes, or until it is bubbly and hot all the way through. Do not overcook, or it will get dry on top.

Serving suggestion: Serve with green salad and fresh fruit and brownies for dessert.

CHILI

This is very good the next day, which means you can cook it a day ahead. It will also be delicious for a second meal. It can be frozen easily if you have some left over. Let it cool and pour into plastic containers with tight-fitting lids. Chili will keep for 6 weeks in the freezer.

Serves: 6

Preparation time: 15 minutes

Cooking time: 30 minutes or more

What you will need:

1 large onion, peeled and chopped
1 clove garlic, peeled and chopped
1 green pepper, cored, seeded, and chopped
2 tablespoons butter, margarine, oil or bacon
   fat
1½ pounds ground beef
salt (1 teaspoon or more)
pepper (¼ teaspoon or more)
2 tablespoons chili powder (or more,
   according to taste)
2 cups canned tomatoes
1 can (about 2 cups) red kidney beans

Add if you like:

½ teaspoon cumin
½ teaspoon basil
½ teaspoon oregano

a large, heavy frying pan

How to cook it:

1. Cook chopped onion, green pepper, and garlic in the butter, margarine, or oil until they start to look transparent (5–10 minutes).

2. Add the ground beef, salt, pepper, chili powder, and basil, oregano and cumin, if you use them. Then add the tomatoes. Stir everything together and cook slowly uncovered for 20–30 minutes. Then taste for seasoning, and add more salt, chili powder, cumin, basil, or oregano if you like it

spicier. Add the cumin and chili powder carefully and in small amounts, as they are hot.

3. 10 minutes before you are ready to serve, add the beans. Stir thoroughly and heat.

Serving suggestions: Serve this with rice (cooked according to package directions) and a salad. Or, instead of rice, serve bread or good crackers. Syrian pita bread, opened up, slightly buttered and toasted in a 350° oven for 10 minutes is delicious, too.

CUBAN PICADILLO

For an unusual and delicious meal for 6 people, which you can prepare ahead of time and warm up at the last minute, serve this Cuban dish with plain white rice and a pot of black beans (see p. 53) for sauce. The beans can be prepared a day ahead. The picadillo and rice can be prepared 3 or 4 hours ahead and reheated. For an extra garnish, slice 3 bananas into diagonal slices, cook gently in butter for 10 minutes, and serve with the picadillo.

Serves: 6

Preparation time: 15 minutes

Cooking time: 45 minutes–1 hour

What you will need:

1 medium onion, peeled and chopped
½ green pepper, seeded, cored, and chopped
1 tablespoon cooking oil
1½ pounds ground beef
1 medium can tomatoes (about 2 cups),
  undrained
salt (1 teaspoon or more)
pepper (¼ teaspoon)

a large, heavy frying pan

How to cook it:

1. Cook the onion and green pepper in the oil over medium heat until they look transparent. Add the beef and cook it, stirring, until it loses its pinkness. Add the tomatoes and salt and pepper. Stir it together, and cook gently over low heat for 45 minutes or longer. If there is too much liquid in the pan, drain some of it off. There should be very little liquid when you are finished.

2. Cook six cups of white rice according to package directions (it takes about half an hour) .

Serving suggestion: Serve the picadillo with rice and the bananas and black beans.

BLACK BEANS

Soak the beans overnight in cold water that comes 2 to 3 inches above the beans. They will swell, so put them in a fairly large pot.

Serves: 6

Preparation time: 10 minutes

Cooking time: 2 hours

What you will need:

2 cups dried black beans, called turtle beans
1 hambone, or ½ pound of ham
(smoked ham, or a small ham hock is good.
If you use a large slice, cut it into 3 or 4
pieces)
1 bay leaf
1 teaspoon salt
1 medium onion, peeled and chopped
½ green pepper, seeded and chopped
1 clove garlic, peeled and chopped
1 tablespoon oil
½ teaspoon thyme
1–2 tablespoons vinegar (any kind will do)

a good-sized pot for beans (4–5-quart size)
a frying pan

How to cook it:

1. Put the presoaked beans in the pot with the hambone or ham, add bay leaf and salt and cover with cold water. Bring to a boil, turn down the heat and cook gently until beans are tender (about 2 hours). Add more water to keep the level just above the beans.

2. While the beans are cooking, cook the chopped onion, pepper, and garlic in the oil in a frying pan. Add the thyme and cook slowly until the vegetables are soft, about 15 minutes.

3. When the onion and pepper are soft, stir in the vinegar, and then add them to the black beans. Taste for seasoning and add salt and pepper to your taste. Add more vinegar if you like.

4. Be careful to stir the beans now and then so that they won't stick to the bottom of the pot.

Serving suggestion: Serve with picadillo, bananas, and lots of plain white rice. Orange sherbet would be good for dessert.

MEAT LOAF

Preparation time: 15 minutes to preheat the oven and mix the ingredients

Cooking time: 1½ hours

What you will need:

1½ pounds ground beef
¾ cup oatmeal (uncooked)
1 small onion, chopped
1½ cups canned tomatoes (save the liquid for
    later)
1 teaspoon salt
¼ teaspoon pepper
2–3 strips bacon

a baking dish, about 2 inches deep, 12 inches
    long, and 7 or 8 inches wide
a large bowl for mixing

How to cook it:

1. Preheat oven to 350°.

2. Put the meat, oatmeal, chopped onion, tomatoes, salt, and
   pepper into the bowl. Mix them together very well, using
   a fork and, if you need to, your hands. Shape it into a loaf,
   and put it in the baking dish. Spread the two strips of
   bacon along the top of the loaf. Put the meat loaf in the
   oven and bake for 1¼ hours.

3. Take the baking dish out of the oven (remember to use
   potholders) and using a spoon or bulb baster, take out of
   the dish as much of the fat as you can (put it into an empty
   can), tilting the dish so that the fat runs into one corner

and is easier to take out. When you have removed as much as you can (there will be a little left) pour the liquid from the canned tomatoes over the meat. Put the meat loaf back into the oven for another 15 or 20 minutes.

Serving suggestion: Put baked potatoes into the oven when you put in the meat loaf. A green salad and apple brown Betty would be good with this. (You could cook the brown Betty at the same time, but make sure you have room in the oven if you plan on doing this).

POT ROAST

This needs long, slow cooking. You can use the leftovers the next day. 4 pounds of meat (which is the amount you need for a pot roast) makes about 8 servings. Heat up the leftovers the next day or use them with rice or in shepherd's pie.

Preparation time: 15 minutes

Cooking time: 3 hours

What you will need:

1 4-pound piece of beef (rump or bottom
round are best, but chuck is good too)
4 tablespoons of butter, margarine, oil or
bacon fat

½ cup of flour
½ teaspoon salt
¼ teaspoon pepper
1 medium onion, peeled and chopped
1 clove of garlic, peeled and chopped
½ teaspoon thyme (¼ teaspoon if powdered)
½ teaspoon ginger
3 cups canned tomatoes and their liquid

a large, heavy pot with a lid, such as a Dutch oven

How to cook it:

1. Chop the onion and garlic. Wipe the meat with a damp cloth.

2. Mix together the flour, salt, and pepper and spread them on a piece of wax paper. Roll the meat in it until it has flour all over it.

3. Heat the fat in the pot and brown the meat in it over medium heat, turning it so that it is evenly browned. This will take 20 to 30 minutes. If the butter or margarine begins to burn a little, add a spoonful or two of oil.

4. When the meat has browned, take it out of the pot with a long fork and set it on a plate for a minute while you pour out the fat into a can. Leave just a tablespoon or two of fat in the pot. (If it has burned, pour it all out and wipe the pan with a large piece of paper towel. Be careful not to burn yourself. Put in two new tablespoons of fat. Now

put in the meat, the onions, and the garlic. Stir the onions and garlic until they are lightly browned, and then add the tomatoes, thyme, and ginger. Cover the pot and cook over low heat for 2½ hours, or until a sharp fork pierces the meat easily. Add ¼ cup water if it begins to stick or burn.

Serving suggestions: This is especially good with mashed potatoes, peas or carrots and perhaps fruit in syrup for dessert. Or try serving egg noodles with it instead of the mashed potatoes.

BOILED BEEF

This is a one-pot meal. It takes long, slow cooking, but very little work. The vegetables can be cooked right in the pot with the meat during the last 30 or 40 minutes. Next day the broth and leftover meat can be used to make a delicious soup, either with thin noodles, or with vegetables (see recipe for vegetable soup, p. 5). It tastes even better if you cook it at least halfway the day before and finish cooking it the next day, adding the fresh vegetables toward the end. The meat should feel tender when pierced with a sharp fork.

Planning your time: Plan on 3 hours. The beef can be cooked a few hours ahead and reheated. Allow about 40 minutes from the time you put in the fresh vegetables until it is ready to serve.

Preparation time: 15 minutes for the meat and first few vegetables. Prepare the other vegetables later, allowing about 30 minutes.

Cooking time: 2–3 hours

What you will need:

1 fresh brisket of beef (4–5 pounds) with as
    little fat as possible on it
1½ teaspoons salt
½ teaspoon pepper
1 teaspoon thyme (½ teaspoon if powdered)
1 onion, peeled
1 bay leaf

2 stalks celery with leaves, rinsed	The easiest way is to buy a package of "soup vegetables" at the store—it will include all of these vegetables and the parsley; be sure to rinse everything and peel the carrot and parsnip.
3 carrots, peeled	
1 sprig parsley, rinsed	
1 leek, split and well rinsed	
1 parsnip	

vegetables to add later:
4 medium potatoes, peeled and cut in quarters
8 carrots, peeled and cut in half
1 small head of cabbage, cut in quarters
1 large can tiny green peas or 1 package
    frozen peas

a large, heavy pot with a lid, such as a Dutch
    oven

How to cook it:

1. Rub the brisket with ½ teaspoon salt, the pepper, and the thyme. Put it in the pot with the onion, carrots, celery, parsley, leek, bay leaf, and enough cold water to cover it. Bring it to a boil, skim the foam off the top with a large spoon, and add 1 teaspoon salt. Put the lid on partway, so that the pot is not completely covered. Cook it over low heat for 2 hours, or until a sharp fork goes easily into the meat (it could take as long as 3 hours) .

2. After 2 hours, test the meat every 10 or 15 minutes with a sharp fork, and when it is almost tender, add the potatoes, carrots and cabbage, cut up. Now cover the pot tightly and cook over medium heat for 30 minutes. Check the vegetables with a sharp fork after they have been cooking for 20 minutes. If they are almost tender, put in the canned or frozen peas and cook for 10 more minutes.

3. Arrange the vegetables on one platter and the meat on another, or put them all on one big platter, if you prefer. Put a cup or two of the broth into a pitcher or bowl and pass it with the meat. The meat should be sliced crosswise against the grain, so that it doesn't fall apart.

Serving suggestion: Dill pickles, brown mustard, and horse-radish go well with this dish. With so many vegetables you do not need a salad. Hot gingerbread with whipped cream would be a perfect dessert for this meal.

BEEF STEW

Serves: 4–6

Preparation time: 40 minutes

Cooking time: 2 hours

What you will need:

3 pounds beef cut up for stew (chuck, round,
  or rump—with fat trimmed off)
1 cup flour
salt and pepper
4 tablespoons butter or margarine
1 tablespoon oil
½ teaspoon thyme
1 onion, peeled and chopped
3 cups liquid (water, or bouillon made with
  water and bouillon cubes)
1 bay leaf
1 stalk celery with leaves
parsley

Add if you like:

6 potatoes, peeled and quartered
6 carrots, peeled and quartered
1 cup green beans, cut in pieces
1 box frozen peas (add last 15 minutes)

heavy kettle such as a dutch oven or
  casserole with a lid

How to cook it:

1. Put the flour in a plastic bag and shake the meat pieces in it, holding the top shut. Shake off the extra flour. Heat the butter and oil in the heavy pot and brown the meat in it, a few pieces at a time. Turn them so they brown on all sides. Sprinkle the meat with salt, pepper, and thyme.

2. Add the liquid and the bay leaf, onion, celery, and parsley. Cook for about 2 hours, until meat is tender.

3. If you like vegetables in your stew, add carrots, potatoes, and small onions 45 minutes before you think the meat will be done. Add green beans and frozen peas 20 minutes before the end.

4. Taste vegetables and meat to make sure they are done and have enough salt and pepper. You can add 1 teaspoon Worcestershire sauce or 1 tablespoon vinegar if you want more seasoning.

Serving suggestions: Serve noodles with this, if you prefer, and leave the potatoes out of the stew. It is also good with mashed potatoes or rice instead of the potatoes in the stew.

IRISH LAMB STEW

This is simple and filling. It is quick to prepare and needs very little watching while it cooks. To feed more people, just add more meat, potatoes, and onions: 1 onion, 1 medium potato, and ¾ pound meat per person.

Serves: 4–5

Planning your time: Allow about 2 hours, including 15 minutes to preheat the oven.

Preparation time: 15 minutes

Cooking time: 1½–2 hours

What you will need:

3 pounds lamb shoulder, cut up for stew
4 medium potatoes, peeled and sliced
4 medium onions, peeled and sliced
salt (about 2 teaspoons)
pepper (about ½ teaspoon)
1 teaspoon thyme
1 leek (if available)
1 stalk celery
¼ cup chopped parsley
1 bay leaf
water to cover the meat

Add if you like:

6 carrots, peeled and cut in large chunks
1 can of peas, drained, *or* 1 package frozen
   peas

an oven-proof casserole with lid

How to cook it:

1. Preheat oven to 350°.

2. Put a layer of meat in the casserole. Cover it with a layer of sliced potatoes, and then a layer of sliced onions. Sprinkle it with ½ teaspoon salt, ½ teaspoon thyme, and ¼ teaspoon pepper. Keep repeating the layers until the meat, potatoes, and onions are used up. Add the leek, celery, parsley, and bay leaf, and just enough water to come to the top of the meat. Cover the casserole and bake it for 1½–2 hours. Test the meat with a sharp fork after 1½ hours.

3. If you add carrots, put them in with the potatoes and onions.

4. If you add peas, add them on top and just heat them up with the stew 15 minutes before serving.

5. If you add more meat and potatoes, don't forget to add more salt and pepper. In any case, taste for seasoning before you serve.

Serving suggestion: Serve this with a green salad.

PORK SHOULDER, CHINESE STYLE

This tastes even better if you cook it at least partly the day before.

Planning your time: This takes about 2–2½ hours. You can cook it early in the afternoon (or a day ahead) and heat it up when you're ready to use it. The noodles can be cooked in the last 20 minutes.

Serves: 4

Preparation time: 10 minutes

Cooking time: 2½ hours

What you will need:

> 1 pork shoulder, 3–4 pounds
> 1 clove garlic, peeled and cut into slivers or a
>   little fresh ginger, if you can get it, peeled
>   and cut into slices
> ½ cup cooking sherry (if you can get it)
> ½ cup soy sauce
> 2 cups cold water
> 1 tablespoon sugar
>
> a pot big enough to hold the meat

How to cook it:

1. With a sharp knife, slash the rind of the meat in 5 or 6 places and stick a sliver of garlic or fresh ginger into each cut. Put the meat and the cold water into the pot and bring to a boil.

2. When the meat is boiling, add the soy sauce, sugar, and sherry. Lower the heat and cook, covered, gently for one

hour. Turn the meat over after the first hour and cook for one more hour, or until tender when pierced with a sharp fork. If the liquid seems to be getting too low at any time, add more water.

3. When it is done, slice off the rind, put on a platter with a little of the cooking liquid.

Serving suggestion: This is delicious with egg noodles and a salad. Serve baked apples for dessert.

SHEPHERD'S PIE

This is a good way to use leftover meat and/or mashed potatoes. You can also add any leftover cooked vegetables, such as carrots or peas. Or you can make it from scratch, using fresh ground beef and freshly mashed potatoes (see p. 101).

Serves: 4

Preparation time: 40 minutes if you make the mashed potatoes fresh; 15 minutes if they are already made. Have the potatoes ready before you start the meat. Preheat the oven for 15 minutes.

Cooking time: 1 hour in all

What you will need:

    1 small onion, peeled and chopped
    3 tablespoons butter or margarine
    2 pounds ground beef, or 3–4 cups cutup
      leftover meat (beef, veal, pork, or lamb)
    2 tablespoons flour
    ¼ cup water
    ½ teaspoon salt
    pepper
    2 cups mashed potatoes (use 4 medium
      potatoes, if you start from scratch)

Add if you like:

    ½ cup cooked vegetable, such as peas, carrots,
      or mushrooms

    a large frying pan
    a small oven-proof casserole

How to cook it:

1. Preheat oven to 375°.

2. Cook the onion in one tablespoon of butter or margarine in the frying pan over medium heat for 5 minutes. Add the meat and cook it, stirring, until it has browned, 10–15 minutes.

3. Stir in 1 more tablespoon butter or margarine, and when it has melted, sprinkle the flour over the meat and stir it in until it has browned.

4. Add the ¼ cup water, and stir the meat and liquid until it has thickened a bit. Add salt and pepper to your taste and put the meat and gravy into a small oven-proof casserole. Add any leftover vegetables you like.

5. Spread the mashed potatoes over the top of the meat and put a few little pieces of butter on top of that. Bake the shepherd's pie for 30–40 minutes, until it is hot and bubbling.

Serving suggestion: Serve with green peas, salad, and baked apples for dessert.

LEFTOVER MEAT WITH RICE

Almost any meat can be used for this—pork, beef, roast or steak, chicken and turkey, lamb or ham. Cut off the fat (and in the case of chicken and turkey the skin), slice thinly or cut into bite-sized pieces. It makes a very good quick meal.

Preparation time: ½ hour, if you don't have leftover rice (follow instructions for cooking the rice on the package) ; 10 minutes, if you do

Cooking time: 10–15 minutes

What you will need:

cutup leftover meat, about ½ cup per person
cooked rice, about ⅔ cup per person (for 4
    people, 3 cups)
2–3 tablespoons cooking oil
2 tablespoons soy sauce

Add if you like:

2 or 3 scallions, peeled and chopped
1 small onion, peeled and chopped
green peas, if you have any left over

a heavy frying pan

How to cook it:

1. Heat 2–3 tablespoons oil in the frying pan. When it is hot,
   brown the meat quickly in it. Add the scallions and onion,
   if you are using them.

2. Add a tablespoon of soy sauce to the meat and stir for a
   minute. Add a bit more oil. Then add the rice, and keep
   stirring it until it is heated through; add more oil, a little
   at a time, if the rice begins to stick to the pan. Add a little
   more soy sauce, to taste. If you have leftover green peas,
   stir them into the meat and rice. (If you use ham, be careful with the soy sauce, as both are salty.) When thoroughly
   heated, remove from heat and serve.

Serving suggestion: A green salad and fresh fruit for dessert
make this an easy meal you can prepare in half an hour.

CHICKEN WITH RICE

This is a one-dish meal, and you can put into it all kinds of things: sausages, ham, shrimp, fish, clams, mussels, and all kinds of vegetables. Once you have made the basic recipe a few times, use your imagination and try some new combinations along with the chicken.

Serves: 6

Planning your time: This can be partly cooked several hours ahead of time or the day before and reheated 20 minutes before you are ready to serve it. If you prepare it ahead, cook it until the rice is *almost* done, about 20 minutes, leaving a little extra liquid in the pan. Don't add the peas until you reheat. Add a little more liquid to the pan if you need it.

Preparation time: 20 minutes

Cooking time: about 1 hour

What you will need:

    3–5 tablespoons cooking oil
    ½ green pepper, chopped
    1 medium onion, peeled and chopped
    1 clove garlic, peeled and chopped
    1 3-pound frying chicken, cut into serving
       pieces
    1 cup ham *or* cooked sausage (Italian sausage
       is good) cut in small pieces

1½ cups rice, uncooked
2 cups canned tomatoes, with liquid
2 cups chicken broth (can be made with
    bouillon cubes)
salt (about 1½ teaspoons)
pepper (¼–½ teaspoons, or to your taste)
1 teaspoon oregano
2 tablespoons vinegar (any kind will do)
1 box frozen peas, thawed, *or* 1 can small
    peas, drained

a large frying pan *or* roasting pan

How to cook it:

1. Heat 3 tablespoons oil in the pan, and cook the onion, green pepper, and garlic in it at medium heat for 5 minutes.

2. Add the chicken pieces and keep turning them until they are lightly browned on all sides (about 15 minutes). Add more oil if you need it.

3. Add the ham or sausage and stir for a minute.

4. Add the rice and stir for a minute, till the grains are coated in oil.

5. Now sprinkle the chicken and rice with ¼ teaspoon pepper and the teaspoon of oregano, and add the tomatoes and the chicken broth. Cover tightly (use aluminum foil if you don't have a lid), lower the flame, and cook for ½ hour, then check the seasoning and add salt and pepper if

necessary. Make sure the rice isn't sticking; add more water or broth if it is. Add the peas and cook for 10 or more minutes or until the rice is done.

Serving suggestion: Serve with sliced tomatoes or green bean salad, and strawberries and cream for dessert.

VEGETABLES

Vegetables should be cooked until just barely tender, which means cooking them just before you are ready to serve them. Most vegetables taste best cooked in a very small amount of boiling salted water, in a pot with a lid. Two cups of water is plenty for most vegetables, with about half a teaspoon of salt. Keep testing the vegetables by tasting them or piercing them with a sharp fork, and serve them the minute they are done. Once they are ready, do not leave them sitting in the cooking water, as they will go on cooking and get mushy. Most vegetables taste best with nothing but salt, pepper, and a tablespoon or two of margarine or butter. Allow $\frac{1}{2}$ to $\frac{3}{4}$ cup of vegetable for each person; 5–6 stalks of asparagus; 2 ears of corn; 1 medium potato or 3 small new potatoes. One medium cauliflower or cabbage serves 4–6 people. One bag of spinach serves 4.

ARTICHOKES

Artichokes can be a separate course. You can begin a meal with them, either hot or cold; or you can serve them cold as a salad course.

Serves: 4

Preparation time: 10 minutes

Cooking time: 30 minutes to one hour

What you will need:

4 large artichokes
4 cups water
1 teaspoon salt
1½ sticks butter, melted
1½ lemons

a large pot with lid
a small pot for melting butter

How to prepare:

1. Cut the stems off the artichokes so they can stand up straight. Wash the artichokes thoroughly under cold running water.

2. Bring the 4 cups of water to a boil in the large pot and add the salt. Set the four artichokes into the pot, cover it, and lower the heat. Cook for 30 minutes and test for doneness with a sharp fork. Cook until tender. When a fork pierces the artichokes easily, take them out of the pot carefully, using a large spoon and fork, and set them upside down on the drainboard of the sink to let the water run out.

3. Melt the butter over low heat, and stir in the juice of the 1½ lemons. Put each hot artichoke right side up in the center of a plate, and divide the butter-lemon mixture into four small dishes, one for each person. Serve as a first course.

To serve cold: Run cold water over the artichokes when they are done. Drain them and chill in the refrigerator. Serve cold on individual plates with small bowls of French dressing (p. 112) at each place. This can be either a first course or a salad course.

ASPARAGUS

Count on at least 6 stalks of asparagus for each person; for medium sized asparagus, buy ½ to ¾ pound per person. It should be well rinsed.

Serves: 4

Preparation time: ½ hour for rinsing and trimming the stalks

Cooking time: about 10 minutes

What you will need:

2–3 pounds of asparagus
2 cups water
½ teaspoon salt
½ stick butter
½ lemon

a large frying pan with lid
a small pot for melting butter

How to cook it:

1. Put the water and salt in the frying pan and put on the lid. Begin heating it over low heat.

2. While the water is heating, prepare the asparagus: break off an inch or two from the ends (it will snap just where the stem begins to be tender), and peel the stalks with a vegetable peeler for 2 or 3 more inches. Rinse very well under running water.

3. When the water in the pan is boiling and the asparagus is trimmed and washed, lay the stalks flat in the boiling water in the pan. Cover the pan and cook over low heat until just barely tender, 10 to 15 minutes. It is very important to keep testing the asparagus, as it will not be good if it gets soft. Use a sharp fork to test it. It should be tender but still firm. Lift the stalks onto a serving dish, using a spatula or two large spoons.

4. While the asparagus is cooking, melt the butter in the small pot. When it has melted, squeeze into it the juice of the lemon half.

5. Pour the butter and lemon juice over the asparagus on the platter, and serve immediately.

BEETS

Beets come in different sizes. The little ones are the tenderest. Allow four very small ones per person, or 2 medium-sized or 1 large. The larger they are the longer they must be cooked. Serve the tiny ones whole, and the larger ones sliced.

Preparation time: none

Cooking time: 30 minutes to an hour, depending on size

What you will need:

   4 tiny, 2 medium, or 1 large beet per person
   3–4 quarts water
   1 tablespoon salt
   2 tablespoons vinegar
   2 tablespoons butter or margarine

   a large pot
   a colander or strainer
   a medium-sized pot for reheating the beets

How to cook:

1. Fill the pot with water up to 3 inches from the top. Cut the tops off the beets leaving 1–2 inches of stems (so the color will not boil out of them when they cook) and put them in the water. Add the salt and vinegar and cook over a medium heat until the beets are tender when pierced with a sharp fork. This will take between ½ hour and an hour, depending on their size.

2. When the beets are done, drain them in the colander and run cold water over them until they are cool enough to handle. Then slip their skins and stems off with your fingers; they should come off easily. If there are any bits of skin that will not come off, cut them off with a sharp knife.

3. Slice the medium-sized or large beets, and heat them up in a pot with the butter or margarine. Sprinkle with salt and pepper, and when they are hot again, serve immediately. For tiny beets, do the same thing, but do not slice them. Sprinkle with chopped fresh dill or parsley if you like.

BROCCOLI

Serves: 4

Preparation time: 5 minutes

Cooking time: about 20 minutes

What you will need:

    1 large bunch broccoli, about 2 pounds
    2 cups water
    1 teaspoon salt
    4 tablespoons butter, melted

a large pot with lid
a colander or strainer
a small pot

How to prepare:

1. Melt the butter in the small pot. Heat the water in the large pot and add the salt.

2. Cut the bottom 3 inches of stalk from the broccoli and pull off most of the leaves. Rinse well in cold water. When the water in the pot is boiling, add the broccoli, cover the pot and lower the heat. Cook for 10 minutes and then test for doneness with a sharp fork. As soon as the broccoli is tender (it will probably be 10 to 15 minutes), drain it in the colander, then put into a large bowl and pour the melted butter over it. Add a squeeze of lemon juice if you like, and sprinkle with salt and pepper. Serve immediately.

Variation: Instead of melting the ½ stick of butter in a small pot, melt 1 stick of butter in a small frying pan and stir in ½ cup dried bread crumbs. Pour it over the hot drained broccoli and squeeze the juice of half a lemon over that. Serve immediately.

BRUSSELS SPROUTS

Serves: 4

Preparation time: 10 minutes

Cooking time: about 15 minutes

What you will need:

1 quart basket (1 pound) brussels sprouts
2 cups water
½ teaspoon salt
2 tablespoons butter or margarine
½ lemon

a medium-sized pot with lid
a colander or strainer

How to cook them:

1. Bring the water to a boil in the pot and add the salt.

2. Trim the stems of each sprout, and peel off any wilted leaves. Cut out any dark spots. Rinse in the colander under cold water, and put into the pot as soon as the salted water has come to a boil. Cover, turn down the heat and cook for 10 minutes. Test for doneness by piercing with a sharp fork. It may take a few more minutes.

3. As soon as the sprouts are done, drain them in the colander and put them into a bowl with the butter or margarine.

Squeeze half a lemon over them and sprinkle with salt and pepper. Serve immediately.

CABBAGE

Serves: 4–6

Preparation time: 10 minutes

Cooking time: 5–10 minutes

What you will need:

1 medium-sized head of cabbage, 2–3 pounds
2 cups water
1 teaspoon salt
4 tablespoons butter or margarine, melted
    (½ stick)
1 tablespoon vinegar

a large frying pan with lid
a colander or strainer
a small pot

How to cook it:

1. Trim off the stalk of the cabbage and cut off the outside leaves which may be a little wilted. Trim off any dark

spots. Then, with a large sharp knife cut the cabbage in half; then slice each half into thin slices, which will fall into shreds. When the cabbage is all sliced, put the shreds into the colander and run cold water over them for five minutes.

2. While you are rinsing the cabbage, bring the 2 cups of water to a boil in the frying pan and add the salt. When the water boils, add the shredded cabbage, lower the heat, and cover the pan. Cook for about 5 minutes or until just tender. Stir once or twice during this time so that it will cook evenly.

3. Melt the butter in the small pot.

4. When the cabbage is done, drain it in the colander, put it into a large bowl, and pour the melted butter over it. Sprinkle salt and pepper on it and add a tablespoon of vinegar. Serve immediately.

CARROTS

Serves: 4

Preparation time: 20 minutes

Cooking time: 15 minutes

What you will need:

3 cups carrots, with tops cut off, peeled and
   sliced. This will take 1 to 1½ bunches
2 cups water
3 tablespoons butter or margarine
½ teaspoon salt
1 teaspoon sugar

a 1-quart pot with lid
a colander or strainer

How to cook them:

1. Cut the tops off the carrots, peel them, and slice them.

2. Bring the 2 cups of water to a boil. Add the salt, sugar, and
   1 tablespoon butter or margarine. Cover the pot, lower the
   heat and cook for 10–15 minutes, or until just tender.
   Drain in a colander and put into a bowl with the remaining 2 tablespoons of butter or margarine, and a sprinkling
   of salt and pepper. Serve immediately.

CAULIFLOWER

Serves: 4–6

Preparation time: none

Cooking time: 20–25 minutes

What you will need:

   1 head of cauliflower, about 2 pounds
   3 cups water
   1 teaspoon salt
   4 tablespoons butter (½ stick), melted

   a large pot with lid
   a small pot

How to cook it:

1. Bring the water to a boil in the large pot and add the salt. Melt the butter in the small pot.

2. While the water is coming to a boil, trim the stem and outer leaves off the cauliflower and cut out any brown spots. Rinse it under running water.

3. When the water is boiling, add the trimmed cauliflower, stem side down. Cover the pot, lower the heat, and cook for 20–25 minutes. Pierce it with a sharp fork after 20 minutes. As soon as the fork goes in easily, the cauliflower is done.

4. With the long fork and a big spoon, gently lift the cauliflower out of the pot and put it on a serving platter. Pour the melted butter over it and squeeze a little lemon juice over that. Sprinkle it with a little salt and pepper. Serve immediately.

Variation: Instead of pouring melted butter over the cauliflower, melt 1 stick of butter in a small frying pan and stir in ½ cup dried bread crumbs. Spread over the top of the cooked cauliflower and serve immediately. You can squeeze half a lemon over the toasted crumbs, if you like.

CORN ON THE COB

Corn on the cob should not be husked until just before you cook it, or it will dry out. Keep it in the refrigerator if you can until then.

Preparation time: 10–15 minutes to boil water and husk the corn

Cooking time: 10–15 minutes

What you will need:

  1 or 2 ears of corn for each person (ask ahead
     if you can how many each one can eat)
  water (3 or 4 quarts or more)
  1 tablespoon salt

  a large pot with lid

How to cook it:

1. Fill the pot with water to about 3 inches below the top. Add the salt and bring the water to a boil.

2. While the water is coming to a boil husk the corn. When it boils, put the corn into the pot and watch it carefully. The minute the water boils *again,* turn off the heat and put on the lid. The corn will be done in exactly five more minutes, but if necessary, it can stay in the water for another 5 minutes if you do not serve all of it at once. Do not leave it in any longer than that, or it will lose its flavor. Put it into a bowl and cover with a clean cloth napkin or dish towel to keep it warm. Serve immediately.

GREEN BEANS

Serves: 4

Preparation time: 20 minutes for trimming beans and boiling water

Cooking time: 10–15 minutes

What you will need:

    1½ pounds fresh green beans
    2 cups water

1 teaspoon salt
1 tablespoon butter
salt and pepper to taste
½ lemon if you like

a medium-sized pot with lid
a colander

How to cook them:

1. Put the water and salt in the pot and bring to a boil.

2. While the water is heating, prepare the beans. Cut or break off the ends, and if there are any "strings" when you do this, pull them off. Break the beans in half. Cut off any spots, and throw out any beans that are wilted or very spotted. Put them in the colander and rinse them in cold water.

3. When the water is boiling and the beans are ready, put the beans in the pot and cover them. Cook over medium heat for 10 minutes. Then test the beans for doneness by taking one out, cooling it for a moment, and biting it. If it feels tender but not raw, it is done. If it still tastes raw, continue cooking them, and testing every two minutes until they are done. Do not overcook.

4. When the beans are done, drain them in the colander and put them back into the dry cooking pot with the butter. Toss them for a minute to melt the butter, add salt and pepper to your taste, and serve immediately. Squeeze a little lemon over them at the last minute if you like.

Note: If you want to use them for salad, omit the butter and seasoning at the end, and toss them in ¼ cup French dressing (see p. 112) when they are cool. You can buy extra beans, cook them all, putting butter on the amount you want to eat hot and saving the rest to use cold in salad the next day.

GREEN PEAS AND SNOW PEAS

Serves: 4

Preparation time: For fresh peas, ½ hour. For frozen or canned peas, none

Cooking time: 10 minutes

What you will need:

>   2 pounds unshelled peas or 1 pound snow peas
>   2 cups water
>   ½ teaspoon salt
>   2 tablespoons butter or margarine
>
>   a 1-quart pot with lid
>   a colander or strainer

How to prepare them:

1. Shell the peas, unless they are snow peas, in which case just snap off the ends. Rinse snow peas.

2. Bring the 2 cups of water to a boil. Add the salt and the peas. Cover the pot, lower the heat, and cook 5–10 minutes. Check after 5 minutes to see if they are done. Snow peas may be done in 3–5 minutes. Check after 3 minutes. Drain in a colander and put into a bowl with 2 tablespoons butter or margarine, a sprinkling of salt and pepper, and a squeeze of lemon juice, if you like. Serve immediately.

Note: If you use canned peas, you will need 2 large cans for 4–6 people. Just heat over low flame for 10 minutes, drain and serve as above. For frozen peas, 2 packages will serve 4–6 people. Follow the directions on the package.

SAUERKRAUT

Sauerkraut usually comes in cans or plastic bags. It must be thoroughly rinsed and pressed dry before you cook it. Put it in a colander and let cold water run through it for a few minutes, then squeeze dry with your hands. It can either be cooked in a covered pot with liquid, or in an uncovered skillet with a little fat in it. Either way, it tastes best when cooked for quite a long time.

Steamed Sauerkraut

Serves: 4

Preparation time: 10 minutes to rinse the sauerkraut and chop the onion (and apple, if you use it)

Cooking time: about 1 hour

What you will need:

> 1 large can sauerkraut, or 2 medium cans
> 1 cup water (or beer, if you like) or a little
>   more
>
> Add if you like:
>
> 1 small onion, peeled and chopped
> 1 small apple, peeled, cored and chopped
>
> If you want to make a meal:
>
> 8 frankfurters or 4 knockwurst (fat frankfurters)
> 4 medium potatoes, peeled and cut into quarters
>
> a large pot with lid

How to cook it:

1. Drain the sauerkraut in the colander and rinse well. Squeeze it dry and put into the pot, along with the cup of water or beer and the chopped onion and apple (if you use them). Put the lid on and cook over low heat for an hour.

   If you want to make an easy meal, add the frankfurters or knockwurst and the cut-up potatoes after the sauerkraut has cooked for 40 minutes. Put them right on top of the sauerkraut. Add a little more water or beer if it looks too dry. Cover the pot and serve as soon as the potatoes are done. This will take about 30 minutes. Prick the frankfurters with a fork once or twice.

Serving suggestion: Serve with mustard and pickles and rye or pumpernickel bread, if possible. Apple brown Betty for dessert would be good.

Pan-Cooked Sauerkraut

Serves: 4

Preparation time: 5 minutes to rinse and drain the sauerkraut

Cooking time: about 1 hour

What you will need:

> 1 large can or 2 medium cans sauerkraut
> 2–3 tablespoons bacon fat, butter, margarine
>   or cooking oil

> Add if you like:

> 1 small onion, peeled and chopped
> 1 small apple, peeled, cored and chopped

> If you want to make a meal:

> 8 frankfurters or 4 knockwurst (fat frankfurters)
> 4 medium potatoes, peeled and cut into
>   quarters

a medium-sized pot for boiling potatoes

a large, heavy frying pan
a colander

How to cook it:

1. Rinse and drain the sauerkraut in the colander.

2. Heat the oil or fat in the frying pan over medium heat and add the onion and/or apple, if you use them. Cook for 2 minutes, then add the drained sauerkraut. (If you do not use the onion or apple, just put the drained sauerkraut into the hot fat in the pan.) Stir and cook for 10 minutes until everything is mixed together—the fat, sauerkraut, onion, and apple. Turn the heat down very low and cook, stirring now and then, for about 45 more minutes. If it begins to burn, add ¼ cup water.

3. If you want to make a meal of it, push the sauerkraut to one side of the pan after it has cooked for half an hour, and add the frankfurters. (If there is not enough room, you can boil them separately for 15 minutes.) Boil the potatoes in a separate pot for 15–20 minutes, and as soon as they are tender combine with sauerkraut and meat.

Serving suggestions: Serve everything together on one platter with mustard and pickles on the side. Have good dark bread, like rye or pumpernickel, and serve an apple dessert.

If you do not cook frankfurters and potatoes with it, sauerkraut is good with roast duck, baked ham, or any kind of pork.

SPINACH

Serves: 4

Preparation time: 10 minutes for washing leaves and removing tough stems

Cooking time: 5–10 minutes

What you will need:

1 cellophane bag of spinach (this makes 4
  smallish servings. Use two bags if you are
  feeding 4 spinach-lovers)
1 tablespoon butter
½ lemon

a large pot with lid
a colander

How to cook it:

1. Wash the spinach leaf by leaf, breaking off any tough stems or brown spots. Put it in the colander as you rinse it.

2. Put the wet leaves into the pot. Cover and cook over low heat for 5 to 10 minutes, or just until the spinach has wilted to the bottom of the pot. Do not overcook.

3. Pour off most of the liquid in the pot and put the spinach in a bowl with the butter and a squeeze of lemon. Sprinkle with salt and pepper and serve immediately.

SUMMER SQUASH AND ZUCCHINI

Serves: 4

Preparation time: 5–10 minutes

Cooking time: 10–15 minutes

What you will need:

> 2 pounds yellow squash or zucchini (about 1 small
>   squash per person)
> 2 cups water
> ½ teaspoon salt
> ¼ teaspoon pepper
> 2–3 tablespoons butter or margarine
> ½ lemon
>
> a 2-quart pot with lid
> a colander or strainer

How to prepare it:

1. Scrub the squash or zucchini with a stiff brush or plastic
   scrubber. Cut off the ends and slice. Summer squash should
   be in rather thick slices, about ½ inch, and zucchini
   should be sliced quite thin, as it is much firmer.

2. Bring the water to a boil and add the salt. Add the sliced
   squash or zucchini, cover the pot, lower the heat, and cook
   for 5–10 minutes, or until tender when pierced with a
   sharp fork.

3. Drain in the colander, put into a serving bowl, with the butter or margarine, and sprinkle with salt and pepper. Squeeze a little lemon juice over it if you like.

Variation: Slice the squash or zucchini. Melt $\frac{1}{2}$ stick butter or margarine in a frying pan with a lid. Add the vegetable, cover the pan, and cook over low heat for 10–15 minutes. When tender, sprinkle with salt (about $\frac{1}{2}$ teaspoon) and pepper (about $\frac{1}{4}$ teaspoon) to taste, add a squeeze of lemon juice if you like, and serve immediately. Pour the butter and juices from the pan over the vegetable.

BAKED TOMATOES

Serves: 4

Baked tomatoes are a nice change from raw ones. They are especially good with roasts, such as lamb or beef, or with lamb chops.

Preparation time: 15 minutes including preheating oven

Cooking time: 20 minutes

What you will need:

    4 medium-sized tomatoes
    salt and pepper

1 teaspoon dried basil, if you like
1 stick butter or margarine
1 cup dried bread crumbs
1 tablespoon cooking oil

a medium-sized pot for melting butter
a baking pan or oven-proof dish to hold four
   tomatoes

How to cook them:

1. Preheat oven to 375°.

2. Melt the butter in the pot, then stir in the bread crumbs
   and remove from the heat.

3. Cut a thick slice off the top of each tomato, removing the
   core. Sprinkle each tomato with salt, pepper, and a pinch
   of basil. Then spread $\frac{1}{4}$ of the buttered bread crumbs on
   each tomato.

4. Rub the baking pan or dish with the tablespoon of oil and
   put in the four tomatoes. Bake for 15–20 minutes. Serve
   immediately.

BAKED CHERRY TOMATOES

Preparation time: 15 minutes for preheating oven

Cooking time: 15–20 minutes

What you will need:

1 small basket cherry tomatoes
2 tablespoons cooking oil or olive oil

Add if you like:

1 garlic clove, peeled and cut in half
1 teaspoon dried basil
salt and pepper

a colander
a baking pan or oven-proof dish

How to cook them:

1. Preheat oven to 375°.

2. Pull the stems off the tomatoes and put them in the colander. Rinse them.

3. Pour the oil into the baking dish and put in the cherry tomatoes. Stir them around with a spoon or your hand for a minute so that they are all coated with the oil. Sprinkle with salt and pepper and bake for 20 minutes.

   If you like a faint taste of garlic, rub the oiled dish with the cut garlic clove before you put it into the oven. If you want to season the tomatoes with the dried basil, sprinkle it over them before you bake them.

POTATOES

Potatoes are everybody's favorite vegetable, and one reason is that they can be cooked so many different ways. Here are a few:

Boiled Potatoes

Preparation time: 15 minutes to boil the water and peel the potatoes

Cooking time: about 20 minutes, depending on size

What you will need:

> 1 medium potato for each person; if you use
>   small red or light brown new potatoes,
>   allow 2 or 3
> 1 tablespoon salt
> 2–3 tablespoons butter or margarine
> chopped parsley, if you want to add it
>
> a large pot
> a colander or strainer

How to cook them:

1. Fill the pot about ⅔ full of water, add a tablespoon of salt, bring it to a boil.

2. While the water is heating, prepare the potatoes. If you use large potatoes, peel them and cut into quarters. If you

use little new potatoes, scrub them but leave the skins on, unless they are very spotty. Their thin skins are delicious tasting and look nice, besides. Put the peeled potatoes into cold water until you are ready to boil them. Otherwise they will turn brown. When you are ready to cook them, put them into the pot of boiling water and cook for about 20 minutes. You will have to keep testing them with a sharp fork, because the cooking time depends on the size of the potatoes.

3. When a sharp fork goes into them easily, drain them in the colander, then put them back in the hot dry pot in which they cooked, along with the butter or margarine. Toss the potatoes and butter together for a minute till the butter melts. Put them into a bowl sprinkle with chopped parsley if you like, and serve right away. Chopped fresh dill is good, too.

Note: Leftover boiled potatoes can be used to make home-fried potatoes.

Mashed Potatoes

Allow 1 medium potato per person

Serves: 4

Preparation time: 15 minutes to boil the water and peel the potatoes.

Cooking time: 30–35 minutes

What you will need:

>4 medium potatoes
>1 tablespoon salt
>5 tablespoons butter or margarine
>about ¼ cup milk or cream, or a little more
>salt
>pepper
>a medium-sized pot
>
>a colander
>a potato ricer or masher
>large spoon or eggbeater

How to cook them:

1. Fill the pot ⅔ full with water, add 1 tablespoon salt and bring to a boil.

2. Peel the potatoes, cut them into quarters or smaller pieces (this will make them a little easier to mash) and put them into the boiling water. Cook until done.

3. Drain the potatoes in the colander, then hold the ricer over the empty pot and rice them into it; or if you use a masher, put the potatoes in the dry pot and mash them in it. Add 4 tablespoons of the butter, and beat it into the potatoes with the masher or a large spoon. Then add the cream or milk and beat them hard again.

4. Taste the potatoes, and add salt and pepper to your taste. If they are too wet, beat them over low heat for a minute or two. If they are too dry, add a little more milk or cream and beat again. If they are still lumpy, beat them hard with an eggbeater. Heat them for a minute over a low fire, put into a bowl, put the remaining tablespoon of butter or margarine into the top of the potatoes, and serve.

Note: Leftover mashed potatoes may be used in shepherd's pie or they can be used to make potato patties: shape cold mashed potato into patties, dip them in flour and brown them in butter in a frying pan. Turn with a spatula and serve when hot and lightly browned on both sides.

Baked Potatoes

Preparation time: 15 minutes for preheating the oven

Cooking time: 1¼ to 1½ hours for medium to large-sized potatoes

What you will need:

1 medium-sized potato for each person
1 teaspoon cooking oil (if you want to rub the potato skins with it)
butter or sour cream to serve with the baked potatoes

How to cook them:

1. Preheat the oven to 375°.

2. Wash the potatoes well, scrubbing off any dirt on the skins. Rub the skins with a little oil if you like. This will make the skins less dry when the potatoes are cooked.

3. Put the potatoes in the oven and bake for 1¼ to 1½ hours. Be sure to prick the skins several times with a sharp fork to let out the steam—do this after the potatoes have baked for about half an hour. The potatoes are done when the fork pierces them easily. Serve with butter or sour cream.

Roast Potatoes

Preparation time: 15 minutes for preheating the oven

Cooking time: 1 to 1½ hours

What you will need:

   1 medium-sized potato for each person
   butter or oil or fat from roasting meat, about
      1 teaspoon per potato
   salt

   a roasting pan

How to cook them:

1. Preheat the oven to 375°. If you are roasting the potatoes in the pan with meat or poultry, you may leave the oven at whatever temperature your meat recipe calls for.

2. Peel and cut into quarters one medium potato for each person. Put them into the roasting pan with about 1 teaspoon butter, margarine, or oil for each potato. After about half an hour, turn the potatoes and salt them lightly. They will be done in about an hour, but can cook longer if you want them browner. If you are roasting meat or poultry, put them right in the pan with the roast. The fat from the meat will usually be enough to cook the potatoes in, but you may add a little more if they look too dry.

Oven-Fried Potatoes

Preparation time: 15 minutes for preheating the oven and peeling and slicing the potatoes

Cooking time: 30–40 minutes

What you will need:

1 medium-sized potato for each person
1 tablespoon butter, margarine or oil for
   each potato
salt

a large flat baking pan or shallow oven-proof
   dish

How to cook them:

1. Preheat the oven to 400°.

2. Peel and slice one medium-sized potato for each person and put the slices in a large shallow pan or dish with about one tablespoon butter, margarine, or oil for each potato. Stir and turn them several times with a spatula so they will brown evenly, and when they are brown and tender, salt them and serve. Cooking time will be 30–40 minutes.

Pan-Fried Potatoes

Preparation time: 15 minutes for peeling and slicing potatoes

Cooking time: about 20 minutes

What you will need:

> 1 medium-sized potato for each person
> ½ to ¾ stick of butter or margarine, or
> ¼ to ½ cup oil
> salt
>
> a heavy frying pan

How to cook them:

1. Peel the potatoes and slice them fairly thin; if you want to make French fries, slice them thicker and then cut the slices into strips.

2. Heat the fat or oil in the frying pan over medium heat, and cook the potatoes in it, turning several times with a spatula, until they are tender and evenly browned. Drain them on paper towels, salt them, and serve immediately.

Home-Fried Potatoes

Serves: 4

You need leftover boiled potatoes for this.

Preparation time: 5–10 minutes to slice potatoes (and onion, if you use it)

Cooking time: 15 minutes

What you will need:

   3 cups (more or less) sliced boiled potatoes
   3 or 4 tablespoons bacon fat, butter,
      margarine, or oil
   salt

   Add if you like:

   1 small onion, peeled and chopped

   a heavy frying pan

How to cook them:

1. Slice the potatoes and chop the onion, if you use it.

2. Heat the fat in the pan over medium heat. If you use onion, put it in and stir for a minute or two; then add the sliced potatoes and cook, stirring and turning every few minutes, until they are brown on both sides and tender. This will take about fifteen minutes. Add plenty of salt, and pepper, if you like it.

Note: If you use new potatoes, you may want to peel them before slicing to make them look a little neater.

Serving suggestion: These are particularly good for breakfast served with fried eggs, but they taste good with almost anything.

SALADS

You can make a salad out of almost anything—leftover meats, trimmed of fat and cut into pieces, cooked vegetables, cooked rice, hard-boiled eggs, tuna fish, salmon, shrimp. Making a good salad is simple, if you keep certain basic rules in mind:

1. Make sure your salad greens are thoroughly rinsed in cold water and fairly dry. After you have rinsed them, let them drain in a colander and then wrap them in a clean dish-towel or paper towels.

2. If you use leftover meat—roast lamb, veal, beef, chicken, pork, or turkey—make sure that you have cut off all the fat and gristle. Remove the skin and bones and cut the meat into small pieces.

3. Never use anything mushy or soggy. Overcooked vegetables will taste awful in salad. Salads should be chewy and crisp.

4. Make sure your salad dressing is good and has a nice sharp taste. Put the dressing on at the last minute. Do not drown the salad in dressing. It will make a soggy mess. Put on just enough so that you can taste the dressing in each bite. Toss the salad lightly but thoroughly, then taste it. It is better to put on too little dressing at first than too much; you can always add, but you can't take away.

5. Salad tastes better if it isn't too cold. Leave your ingredients out of the refrigerator for half an hour or so before you serve. Cold kills the taste of almost any food.

6. Do not refrigerate your salad dressing and only make enough for a day or two at a time.

7. Once you get used to making salads of the simpler kind, don't be afraid to use your imagination and invent some. Summer is a wonderful time to experiment with tossed salads that make a whole meal.

BASIC FRENCH DRESSING

Serves: 4

Preparation time: 5 minutes

What you will need:

½ cup oil (Use good French or Italian olive oil if
  you can get it. Next best choice is safflower oil)
2½ tablespoons vinegar (wine vinegar, white
  or red, is good, but cider or regular white
  vinegar will do)
a rounded ¼ teaspoon salt
¼ teaspoon pepper (freshly ground is best)
¼ teaspoon dry mustard

Add if you like:

1 clove garlic, peeled and cut in half
1 scallion, chopped

a jar with tight-fitting lid, or a bowl or cup for
mixing

How to prepare it:

1. Measure the oil into the jar or bowl (or mix the dressing
   right in the measuring cup). Add the salt and pepper and
   mustard, cover the jar, and shake well. Then add the vinegar, cover and shake again. (Or, if you use the bowl or cup,
   stir hard with a fork, then add the vinegar and stir hard
   again.

2. Add the cut clove of garlic, if you like the taste, and let it
   sit in the dressing for half an hour, then throw it out. For
   a slightly oniony taste, chop the scallion and put it into
   the dressing a few minutes before you use it.

BASIC GREEN SALAD

Preparation time: 10–20 minutes, depending on how many
ingredients you use

What you will need:

4–5 cups of greens. This may be iceberg lettuce,
   romaine, Boston lettuce, watercress, Bibb
   lettuce, endive, salad bowl lettuce, spinach,
   or escarole, to name a few
¼ to ½ cup French dressing (see p. 112) for
   a salad for four people

Add if you like:

2 tomatoes, cored and cut into quarters or
   eighths
½ avocado, peeled and sliced
1 cucumber, peeled and sliced
½ cup bean sprouts or alfalfa sprouts
1 raw zucchini, scrubbed and sliced
½ cup fresh mushrooms, wiped with a damp
   cloth and sliced
3–4 scallions, chopped

How to prepare it:

1. Wash the salad greens carefully (spinach needs several
   rinsings if you buy it loose; it is less trouble to buy it in
   plastic bags, and give it one good rinsing). Put them in a
   colander to drain, or wrap them in a clean dishtowel to
   absorb the water. Pat them dry with a paper towel. Break
   off tough stems or any brown spots, and break into bite-
   sized pieces.

2. Just before you are ready to serve, put the salad greens
   into a bowl, add the other ingredients, if you are using any,

and toss the salad lightly with French dressing. Do not put too much dressing on the salad, or it will get soggy. Put on just enough to coat each leaf lightly.

Chef's Salad

To a bowl of salad greens, add one cup of cutup, cooked chicken, turkey, or ham, one cup of swiss cheese, cut in small strips, pieces of ripe avocado, quartered tomatoes, and 2 or 3 quartered hard-boiled eggs. You can also add any of the other additional ingredients listed under basic green salad. You can toss this salad with Fresh dressing just before serving, or pass the French dressing separately in a pitcher and let each person take some.

CHICKEN, TURKEY, AND MEAT SALADS

Use leftover meat for this.

Serves: 4

Preparation time: ½ hour

Cooking time: none

What you will need:

2½ cups cooked meat which may be chicken,
    turkey, lamb, ham, beef, pork, or veal
1 cup chopped celery
¼ cup chopped scallions
½ cup mayonnaise
¼ cup sour cream
1 tablespoon brown mustard
juice of ½ lemon
salad greens, rinsed and fairly dry
2 medium tomatoes, cored and cut in quarters

Add if you like:

To the mayonnaise—
2 dill pickles, finely chopped
¼ green pepper, cored, seeded, and chopped

To the salad platter—
3 hardboiled eggs, cut into quarters
1 cucumber, peeled and sliced
olives
radishes (cut off stems)

a large bowl

How to prepare it:

1. Cut off all skin, fat, or gristle from the meat and remove
   bones, if there are any. Cut the meat into bite-sized pieces.
   Place in bowl.

2. Mix the mayonnaise, sour cream, mustard, and lemon
   juice together. Add this dressing to the meat in the bowl.

Add the chopped celery and scallions (and the chopped pickle and/or green pepper, if you like) and mix everything together well with a fork or large spoon. Taste for seasoning, and add salt, pepper, or more mustard or lemon juice, scallions, or pickle, if it seems to need it.

3. Put the washed salad greens on a platter or in a fairly large bowl, and put the meat salad in a mound in the center of it. Decorate with tomato quarters, or any of the other ingredients you choose. Let stand at room temperature for 10 or 15 minutes before serving.

TUNA FISH SALAD

The best tasting tuna is solid white meat, packed in oil, but you can use any other kind. Use 1 small tin of tuna for each person, or 1 medium-sized can for 2 people. This is a mixed tuna fish salad and can be used for sandwiches, or on a plate with lettuce, tomato, and hard-boiled egg (pass French dressing on the side) for a delicious summer lunch. Serve lots of good bread with it.

Serves: 4

Preparation time: 20 minutes

What you will need:

2 medium-sized cans of tuna
½ small onion, peeled and finely chopped
mayonnaise (about ⅓ cup)
juice of 1 lemon

Add if you like:

3 hard-boiled eggs, quartered
3 tomatoes, cut in eighths

How to prepare it:

1. Drain the oil carefully from the cans of tuna. Put tuna in a bowl and mash with a fork.

2. Add the other ingredients (except the eggs and tomatoes) and mix thoroughly.

Serving suggestions: Use in sandwiches, or make a mound of it in the middle of a bowl lined with lettuce. Arrange the tomatoes and hard-boiled eggs around the tuna. Pass a pitcher of French dressing with it.

EGG SALAD

Serves: 4

Preparation time: ½ hour, including 20 minutes to boil and cool the eggs

What you will need:

5 eggs
¼ cup mayonnaise, more or less
1 large tablespoon mustard
1 stalk of celery, rinsed and chopped
1 tablespoon chopped sweet pickle, if you
    have it
salt and pepper to taste
1 teaspoon vinegar

a pot for cooking the eggs
a small mixing bowl

How to prepare it:

1. Boil the eggs for 8–10 minutes, starting them in cold water. Then cool them in cold running water for a minute or two, remove them from the pot and put them in the refrigerator for 10 minutes.

2. While the eggs are cooling, chop the celery and pickle, if you have it.

3. When the eggs are fairly cool, peel them, put them in the mixing bowl, and chop them up into small pieces. Add the mayonnaise, little by little so that you can see just how much you want; add the mustard, the celery, and the pickle, and stir everything lightly together with a fork. Taste for seasoning, and add more mayonnaise or salt or pepper if necessary. Add the vinegar and stir again. If you like it spicier, add a little more mustard.

Serving suggestions: You can use this as sandwich filling, or you can serve it as a salad, by serving it in the center of a bowl of lettuce leaves. Decorate with ripe tomatoes, cut into quarters, and serve with pumpernickel or rye bread and sweet pickles.

BEAN SALAD

Make this an hour or two ahead of time so the beans can absorb the flavor of the dressing. This is very good with cold meat—sliced ham, roast beef, pork, or cold cuts. You can use canned white beans or chick peas, as well as kidney beans, or any combination of beans.

Serves: 4

Preparation time: 20 minutes

What you will need:

1 large can (16-oz.) red kidney beans, drained
2 stalks celery, washed and chopped
1 tablespoon onion, peeled and chopped
4 scallions, chopped
French dressing (see p. 112)
salt and pepper

Add if you like:

1–2 cups canned white beans, drained, can be
mixed with the red. So can cooked green
beans, cut in pieces. You can add more
celery and scallions also

How to prepare it:

Mix everything together lightly in mixing bowl. Season to
taste.

Serving suggestion: Place lettuce leaves on serving platter
and pile the beans on top.

RICE SALAD

Serves: 4

Planning your time: In this case, the main preparation is
cooking the rice, which takes about 30 minutes. After that,
there is no cooking. While the rice is boiling, boil the eggs
and cool them and chop the vegetables.

Preparation time: 40 minutes; 30 minutes for cooking the
rice. Prepare the vegetables and hard boil and cool the eggs
at the same time. Then put everything together.

Cooking time: none

What you will need:

    1 cup uncooked rice
    ½ cup French dressing, but make it with half
        oil and half vinegar (see p. 112 for basic
        recipe)
    ¼ cup chopped scallions
    ¼ cup chopped green pepper (cored and
        seeded)
    ¼ cup chopped celery
    ¼ cup chopped cucumber
    (or any combination of the above four
        ingredients)
    salt and pepper (preferably freshly ground)
        to your taste
    ¼ cup French dressing
    4 eggs

    a pot for cooking rice, with lid

How to prepare it:

1. Cook rice according to package directions. It will take about 30 minutes.

2. While the rice is cooking, boil the eggs until hard, about 10 minutes. Run cold water over them and then put in refrigerator to cool.

3. Mix rice while it is still warm with the ½ cup French dressing that has more vinegar in it than usual.

4. Add ¼ cup each of chopped scallions, chopped green pepper, chopped celery, and chopped cucumber, or any combination of those that you like. Add salt and pepper to your taste, about ½ teaspoon of each.

5. Just before serving, add the additional French dressing, and stir well.

6. Peel the hard-boiled eggs and cut them into quarters. Put them around the edge of the salad. Add one or two tomatoes, cut into quarters, if you like, also.

Serving suggestion: Put some lettuce on a platter and pile the rice in the middle. Then decorate with the tomatoes and eggs. This is very good with cold sliced meat.

COLESLAW

Serves: 4

Preparation time: 20 minutes

What you will need:

1 small head of cabbage *or* ½ large head of
   cabbage
1–2 tablespoons French dressing (see p. 112)
about ½ cup mayonnaise

¼ cup sour cream
2 teaspoons mustard
salt and pepper to taste

How to prepare it:

1. With a large sharp knife (be very careful to keep your fingers out of the way), shred 1 small head of cabbage or ½ a large one as finely as you can.

2. Add about ½ cup mayonnaise, French dressing, the sour cream, and mustard.

3. Mix thoroughly and let stand ½ hour before serving. Season with salt and pepper to your taste.

Note: If you like it sweeter, add a teaspoon or two of sugar and mix very well. You can also grate a carrot into it if you like.

CUCUMBER SALAD

Peel and slice very thinly 1 small cucumber for each person. Put them in a serving dish, and pour French dressing (see p. 112) over them. Let them sit for half an hour before serving, to soak up the dressing.

Sprinkle with chopped fresh dill or dried dill, if you have it. Or, instead of the French dressing, mix ½ cup sour cream with 3 tablespoons French dressing, add some dill and salt, and pour over the cucumbers. Serve this salad very cold.

STUFFED TOMATOES

For a fancy summer lunch or supper, cut the top off large ripe tomatoes, one for each person. Dig out the tomato insides carefully with a spoon, and fill each one with tuna fish salad, or any of the chicken, turkey, or meat salads.

SLICED TOMATOES

These are only really good in the summer, when ripe tomatoes are available. Slice $1/2$ large or 1 whole medium tomato for each person. Slice one red onion very thinly and separate the slices into rings. Put four or five onion rings over each sliced tomato, and pour a little French dressing (see p. 112) over it just before you serve it. Dried or chopped fresh basil is good sprinkled on tomatoes.

VEGETABLE SALAD

Preparation time: 30 minutes for preparing and cooking the vegetables (10 minutes for peeling, 20 minutes for cooking)

Cooking time: none. Just mix with French dressing and let cool

What you will need:

>3 cups of cooked vegetable (green beans,
>   canned beets, sliced boiled potatoes, peas,
>   carrots) or, if you use asparagus, 6 stalks
>   for each person)
>¾ cup French dressing (see p. 112) with 2
>   chopped scallions added
>*or*
>¼ cup mayonnaise, thinned with 2 tablespoons
>   French dressing, with 2 chopped scallions
>   added, may be mixed with any of the above
>   vegetables

How to prepare it:

1. Cook the vegetables in 2 cups water and one teaspoon salt until just tender. Drain in a sieve, run cold water over them and cool in the refrigerator for 10 minutes.

2. Mix with French dressing or mayonnaise and cool in refrigerator for 30 minutes to 1 hour before serving. The

salad should be not quite cold. If the vegetables are left-overs, take them out of the refrigerator one-half hour before serving and mix them with French dressing or mayonnaise. If you serve asparagus, arrange the stalks on each plate and just pour a little dressing over them. Add a squeeze of lemon to the vegetable salad just before serving.

WHITE BREAD

This is fun to make. You will need nearly 5 hours in all to do it, so plan it for a rainy afternoon. A great deal of the time you will be waiting for the bread to rise, so you can be doing something else as well. But bread does need to be watched. It is very satisfying to look at, to smell, and to eat. Wear a large apron to keep the flour off you whenever you're baking.

Preparation time: about 4 hours, including 2 hours waiting time and 15 minutes to preheat oven

Cooking time: 40 minutes

What you will need:

1 package *or* 1 cake yeast
2¼ cups warm milk
2 tablespoons sugar
1 tablespoon salt
6 cups flour
½ stick butter or margarine, melted

a small pan for heating milk
a small pan for melting butter
a large bowl for mixing
2 bread pans, about 9 inches by 5 inches by
   3 inches (buttered)
a rolling pin
a large wooden spoon

How to cook it:

1. Warm the milk in a small pan and pour it into the mixing bowl. Add the yeast, sugar, and salt, and stir until the yeast is dissolved.

2. Stir in 3 cups of flour, a little at a time, mixing well with wooden spoon. When the 3 cups are mixed, add the melted butter and stir again.

3. Add the remaining 3 cups of flour, and mix with spoon until the dough sticks together in a large ball.

4. Sprinkle a little flour on a worktable or counter, put the dough on it, turn the bowl upside down over it, and let it sit for 10 minutes.

5. Uncover the bread after 10 minutes and knead it, pushing your fingers and the heel of your hands into it, folding it over, and turning it, repeating for about 5 minutes, or until the dough is stretchy and smooth.

6. Now put the dough into the bowl again, cover it with a clean dishtowel and put it in a warm corner of the kitchen (on top of an oven that is on very low, or near a hotter one, for instance). Let it sit for about 1½ hours. It will rise until it is twice the size it was when you started.

7. When the dough has doubled, put it on a counter or table, and punch it hard with your fists to knock the gas out of it. You can even pick it up and slap it down hard on the table. Then knead it for 2 or 3 minutes, cut it in half, and put

each piece into a buttered bread pan. Cover them again with a dishtowel, and let them rise in a warm place for about an hour, until they are again nearly twice their original size.

8. While the bread is rising this time, preheat the oven to 375°.

9. This time when the loaves have doubled their size, put them into the oven and bake for about 40 minutes, until they are nicely browned.

Note: Take the loaves out of the pans right away and put them on some sort of rack to cool. (Use a dry dish rack, or a rack taken out of the oven, if you don't have a small metal one. Or just put each loaf across the top of a small bowl, so that it rests on the bowl edges. The idea is to let the air cool and dry the bottom as well as the sides.) Store them in a covered place when they are cool.

You may brush the loaves with melted butter before you bake them, if you like. It will give them a more golden crust, with a buttery taste.

BISCUITS

Preparation time: 30 minutes, including 15 minutes to preheat oven

Cooking time: 10 minutes

What you will need:

> 2 cups of flour
> 2½ teaspoons of baking powder
> 1 teaspoon salt
> 2 teaspoons sugar
> 5 tablespoons butter or margarine
> ¾–1 cup milk (use just enough to make the
>   dough stick together)
>
> a flour sifter or sieve
> a rolling pin
> a bowl
> a cookie sheet

How to cook it:

1. Preheat oven to 450°.

2. Put the flour, baking powder, salt and sugar into the sifter and sift them together into the bowl.

3. Add the butter or margarine and with two table knives or your fingers keep cutting and crumbling the mixture until the butter is mixed with the flour and there are no big lumps left.

4. Stir in the milk slowly, using just enough to make the dough stick together. It should pick up all the flour in the bowl, but not be too sticky to handle. You will probably use about ¾ cup of milk, maybe a little more.

5. Sprinkle a little flour on your worktable, board, or counter, put the ball of dough on it, and knead it for a minute (not too much or the dough will get tough). Press the heels of your hands into the dough, press down with your fingers, fold the dough in half and give it a quarter-turn. Repeat this five or six times. Then rub a little flour on the rolling pin and roll the dough out to ½ inch thickness. Take a small glass and cut out circles of the dough. You should get 12–15 from this recipe.

6. Butter a cookie sheet and put the biscuits on it. Bake at 450° for ten minutes. Let them cool slightly, then serve. Biscuits are best when still warm.

Frankfurters Wrapped in Biscuit Dough (Pigs in a Blanket)

Roll biscuit dough ¼ inch thick, or even a little thinner, and cut out rectangles just big enough to wrap a frankfurter in —about 3 inches wide and 5 or 6 inches long. Put mustard on the frankfurters, put the frankfurters on the dough strips, roll them up, and bake them on a buttered cookie sheet at 400° for about 20 minutes.

CORN BREAD OR MUFFINS

Preparation time: 20 minutes, including 15 minutes to pre-heat oven

Cooking time: 20 minutes

What you will need:

¾ cup corn meal
1 cup flour
⅓ cup sugar
3 teaspoons baking powder
½ teaspoon salt
1 cup milk
1 egg
3 tablespoons butter, melted

an eggbeater
a sieve or flour sifter
2 bowls, 1 small and 1 large
a square baking pan, about 8 inches on each
  side, or muffin tins
a small pot for melting butter

How to cook it:

1. Preheat the oven to 425°.

2. Melt the butter in the small pot.

3. Grease the baking pan or muffin tins with butter or margarine.

4. Break the egg into the small bowl and beat with the egg-beater for a minute.

5. Sift the corn meal, flour, sugar, baking powder and salt into the bowl. Add the milk, egg, and melted butter. Stir with a spoon until everything is very well mixed.

6. Pour into the greased pan or tins. (If you use the muffin tins, they should only be filled to about 3/4 of the way up.) Bake 20 minutes. Let them cool for 10 minutes and then remove the muffins from the tins (they will come out easily) or cut the cornbread into squares. Serve warm, if possible, with butter.

BLUEBERRY MUFFINS OR CAKE

These can also be made as a cake, if the batter is baked in a buttered square pan. Both are delicious for breakfast, tea, or, in cake form, as a dessert.

Preparation time: about 30 minutes, including 15 minutes to preheat oven

Cooking time: 30 minutes; if baked as a cake, 1 hour

What you will need:

1½ cups of sifted flour
2 teaspoons baking powder
½ teaspoon salt
1 cup sugar
1 stick butter or margarine at room
 temperature
1 teaspoon vanilla
1 egg
⅔ cup milk
1½–2 cups fresh blueberries
2 tablespoons flour (besides the cup and a
 half)
1 tablespoon sugar (besides the one cup of
 sugar)

a sieve or flour sifter
a muffin pan or cake pan (9 inches by 9 inches
 by 2 inches)
4 medium-sized bowls

How to cook it:

1. Preheat oven to 350°.

2. Sift the flour into a bowl. Then measure 1½ cups. (You
   will have a little more than you started with. Save the extra
   flour for later.) Into another bowl, sift the cup and a half
   of flour together with the salt and the baking powder.

3. In the third bowl put the stick of butter or margarine, the
   sugar, and the vanilla. Beat it together with a wooden

spoon, pressing on the butter to soften it. This will be hard at the beginning, but as the butter softens and the sugar dissolves into it, it gets easier. Beat it until the mixture is fairly soft and smooth.

4. Into the bowl with the butter-sugar-vanilla mixture gradually stir the flour (1½ cups with the baking powder and salt in it) and the milk. It is easiest if you add a little flour, then a little milk, until you have mixed them all in and the batter is smooth.

5. Now put the blueberries into the fourth bowl. (Make sure they have been rinsed and that most of the stems and leaves have been picked out.) Add the extra 2 tablespoons of flour and 1 tablespoon of sugar to the blueberries, stir them lightly together, and pour the berries into the bowl with the batter. Mix gently but well with a spoon, and spoon the batter into the greased muffin tins or cake pan.

6. Bake the muffins 30 minutes at 350°. For the cake, bake about one hour. Let them cool for a few minutes, then take them out of the muffin tins. If you make cake, cut it into squares and serve. Pass whipped cream with the cake, if you like.

Note: If you can't get blueberries, you can use peeled, chopped apples instead.

BUTTER COOKIES WITH JAM CENTERS

Preparation time: 20 minutes

Cooking time: 10–15 minutes, including 15 minutes to pre-heat oven

What you will need:

> 2 sticks butter (not margarine) at room
>   temperature
> ½ cup sugar
> 2 cups flour
> red jelly or jam such as strawberry, raspberry,
>   currant
>
> a bowl
> a cookie sheet

How to cook it:

1. Preheat oven to 375°.

2. Put the butter and sugar into the bowl, and with a wooden spoon mash and stir them together until the mixture looks smooth and soft.

3. Add the flour, and stir it in until the dough sticks together and is slightly damp. Shape it into balls the size of walnuts, and press your finger into the center of each one, making

a small hollow. Fill the hollow with jelly and bake on un-greased cookie sheets for 10–15 minutes. The cookies will flatten as they bake.

Note: This makes about 4 dozen cookies.

CAROLYN'S GINGER COOKIES

Preparation time: 20 minutes

Cooking time: 10 minutes

What you will need:

   1½ sticks butter or margarine (take it out of
     the refrigerator ½ hour ahead if you can)
   1 cup sugar (white)
   1 egg
   ¼ cup molasses
   2 cups sifted flour
   1 teaspoon salt
   2 teaspoons baking soda
   1 teaspoon ground ginger
   1 teaspoon cinnamon
   1 teaspoon ground cloves
   a little extra sugar

   a large bowl for mixing

a wooden spoon or large mixing spoon
an eggbeater
1 or 2 cookie sheets
a sieve or flour sifter

How to cook them:

1. Preheat oven to 375°.

2. Butter cookie sheet. Sift the flour directly into a 2-cup measuring cup.

3. Break the egg into the bowl. Add the butter, sugar, and molasses, and beat until soft and well-mixed. Begin beating with the spoon, to soften the butter; then mix with the eggbeater.

4. Gradually add the flour, salt, soda, ginger, cinnamon, and cloves; keep stirring with the spoon until it is well mixed and no flour shows.

5. Roll the dough into walnut-sized balls and roll them in the dish of extra sugar. Put them on the greased cookie sheet two inches apart. Bake for 10 minutes. When they are done, let them cool a few minutes, then lift them off the cookie sheet with a spatula.

BROWNIES

Preparation time: 30–40 minutes, including 15 minutes to preheat oven

Cooking time: 25 minutes

What you will need:

2 squares unsweetened baking chocolate
5 tablespoons butter
⅔ cup flour
½ teaspoon baking powder
½ teaspoon salt
2 eggs
1 cup sugar
1 teaspoon vanilla
½ cup chopped walnuts, if you like

a medium-sized pot
an eggbeater
2 bowls, one medium-sized and one large
a square baking pan (about 8 inches by 8
   inches by 2 inches)

How to cook it:

1. Preheat oven to 350°.

2. Grease the baking pan with butter.

3. Put the chocolate and the butter into the pot and melt them together over low heat, stirring once or twice.

4. Put the flour into the smaller bowl, and stir the baking powder and salt into it.

5. Break the eggs into the other bowl, and beat them well for a minute with the eggbeater. Add the sugar little by little and beat after each addition.

6. When the sugar is beaten into the eggs, pour the chocolate and butter mixture into the eggs. (A rubber spatula is good for scraping all the chocolate out of the pot.) Add the vanilla. Then add the flour, and stir well with a spoon, until the mixture looks smooth and no flour shows. Then stir in the nuts, if you use them.

7. Pour the batter into the greased baking pan. Spread it out so it is fairly even. Bake for 25 minutes at 350°. When it is cool, cut it into squares in the pan.

APPLE BROWN BETTY

This has a wonderful buttery taste.

Serves: 4–6

Preparation time: 30–40 minutes, including 15 minutes to preheat oven

Cooking time: 40 minutes

What you will need:

6 slices of bread (any kind)
¾ stick butter, melted
4 cups apples, quartered, peeled, cored, and
   sliced (green or Macintosh apples are best)
½ cup sugar, brown or white
1 teaspoon cinnamon
juice of ½ lemon
½ cup hot water

a medium-sized bowl
a medium-sized pot for melting butter
a baking dish deep enough to hold the apples
   (about 7 or 8 inches across and 3 or 4 inches
   deep)

How to cook it:

1. Preheat oven to 350°.

2. Melt the butter in the pot over low heat. Turn off heat as soon as the butter is melted.

3. While the butter is melting in the pot, begin crumbling the bread into it with your fingers. Stir the butter and crumbs together with a fork so that they are well mixed.

4. Sprinkle half the buttered crumbs over the bottom of the baking dish. Then put half the apples on top of the crumbs.

5. Now mix together the sugar, cinnamon, lemon juice, and hot water, and stir well to dissolve the sugar. Pour half of this mixture over the apples in the dish. Then put the rest of the apples into the dish, pour the rest of the sugar and water over them, and spread the remaining crumbs over the top of the apples. Put it in the oven to bake for 40 minutes.

Serving suggestion: Serve warm, plain, or with cream or vanilla ice cream.

APPLESAUCE

Serves: 4

Preparation time: 30 minutes

Cooking time: about 30 minutes

What you will need:

8 apples (green or Macintosh apples are best)
½ cup water
a pinch of salt
½–¾ cup sugar
1 tablespoon lemon juice
½ teaspoon cinnamon

a medium-sized pot with lid
a medium-sized bowl

How to cook it:

1. Cut the apples into quarters and peel and core them. Keep them in a bowl of cold water until you are ready to use them. This will keep them from turning brown. When they are all peeled and cored, slice them into a pot in which you have put ½ cup of water. Add a pinch of salt, cover the pot and cook over low heat until the apples are soft, about 20–30 minutes. Keep testing them with a fork. Stir them once or twice with a spoon.

2. When the apples are soft, add ½ cup of sugar, the lemon juice, and the cinnamon. Cook for a few minutes and taste them. If they are not sweet enough for you, keep adding sugar in small amounts until it tastes the way you like it. Cook for a few minutes more until all the sugar is dissolved. Stir very well with a fork (you can even use an eggbeater) to make sure the apple slices are well broken up. Do not put through a strainer, or it will taste like baby food.

3. Chill until ready to serve.

BAKED APPLES

This is a delicious, simple dessert.

Preparation time: 15 minutes, including 15 minutes to pre-heat oven

Cooking time: 30–40 minutes

What you will need:

　　1 apple per person (any kind will do)
　　sugar (white or brown), about ¼ cup for 2
　　　apples
　　butter or margarine (1 tablespoon per apple)
　　water (about 2 cups)

　　a baking pan
　　an apple corer

How to cook it:

1. Preheat oven to 350°.

2. Rinse the apples and cut out the cores with an apple corer.
　　(Just press down and keep turning until the core is loose
　　and can be pulled out.) If you don't have a corer, take a

small sharp knife and carefully cut down around the core, then scoop out the core with a teaspoon and the knife. (Be careful that the knife doesn't slip.)

3. Fill the hollow centers of the apples with either white or brown sugar. Press a tablespoon of butter or margarine on top of the sugar in each apple, and put the apples into a baking pan filled with one inch of water.

4. Bake at 350° for about 30–40 minutes.

Serving suggestions: Serve with heavy cream or vanilla ice cream.

DEEP-DISH APPLE PIE

Preparation time: 45 minutes–1 hour, including 15 minutes to preheat oven and 15–20 minutes to mix pastry. Allow 20–30 minutes for peeling and slicing the apples.

Cooking time: 45 minutes

What you will need:

   10 apples, peeled, cored and sliced (green or
      Macintosh apples are best)
   1 cup sugar

2 teaspoons cinnamon
juice of ½ lemon
2 tablespoons flour

a rolling pin
a deep oven-proof dish
1 recipe tart pastry (see p. 159), *or* 1 frozen
   pie shell, thawed for 15 minutes

How to cook it:

1. Make the pastry, unless you are using a frozen pie crust.

2. Preheat oven to 400°.

3. Mix together in the baking dish all the ingredients except
   the pie crust.

4. Rub a little flour on the rolling pin and roll the tart or pie
   pastry out flat on a slightly floured board or table. Spread
   it across the top of the baking dish. If you use a frozen pie
   shell, carefully lay it upside down over the apples. (It will
   easily lift out of its aluminum tin.) Pinch the crust down
   around the edge of the dish, trim off the sides with scissors
   or a knife, cut a few slits in it with a sharp knife, and bake
   for about 45 minutes or until the crust is nicely browned.

Serving suggestions: Serve hot, plain or with vanilla ice
cream or heavy cream.

Cheddar cheese is very good with apple pie, too (but don't
serve it with ice cream and cheese together) .

FRUIT BOWL

You can vary the ingredients for this according to what you have in the house. It is a very good way to make dessert for four people out of odds and ends of fruit, or to use fruit that may have some spots on it but is still good. Plan on 6–8 pieces of fruit for four people.

Serves: 4–6

Preparation time: 20–30 minutes

What you will need:

2 bananas, sliced
2 oranges, peeled and cut into sections
2 apples, peeled and cut up
2 ripe pears, peeled and cut up *or* 1 pear and
    1 grapefruit, peeled and cut into sections
2–3 cups orange juice

Add if you like:

seedless grapes, washed
strawberries, washed, with stems cut off
ripe peaches, peeled and sliced
blueberries, washed and with stems removed

a medium-sized bowl to serve the fruit

How to prepare it: Pour some orange juice into the bowl, and put the fruit into it as you cut it up. The juice will keep it from turning brown. When all fruit is cut up, fill the bowl to almost cover the fruit with more orange juice. Serve in small bowls.

COOKED FRUIT IN SYRUP

This is an easy and delicious dessert that can be served hot or cold, and it makes a wonderful end to almost any meal. You can use whatever fruit is in season—pears, peaches, or plums—but make sure they are firm and not quite ripe.

Pears in Syrup

Preparation time: 20–30 minutes

Cooking time: 20–30 minutes

What you will need:

1 firm pear per person

For the syrup:

1 cup sugar
2 cups water
2 teaspoons vanilla

a large pot with lid

How to cook it:

1. In the pot, stir together the sugar and water and boil over medium heat for fifteen minutes. Add the vanilla.

2. While the syrup is boiling, peel the pears, but leave them whole. Do not remove the stems. After the syrup has boiled for 15 minutes and you have added the vanilla, put the pears, stems up, into the pot. Cover it, and lower the heat. Cook gently for about 20 minutes or until a sharp fork pierces them easily. Test the pears with a sharp fork after 10–15 minutes. Do not overcook.

Serving suggestions: Serve warm or cold, with a little syrup poured over each one. Serve with heavy cream or vanilla ice cream, if you like.

Peaches or Plums in Syrup

Preparation time: 20–30 minutes

Cooking time: 20–30 minutes

What you will need:

2 or 3 fruits per person
syrup, as in the above recipe for pears

a large pot with lid

How to cook it:

1. Make syrup (see recipe for pears in syrup, p. 154).

2. Wash the peaches and peel them with a vegetable peeler. Plums do not need to be peeled. Leave them whole. Put the fruit into the syrup, cover the pot and cook over low heat for about 15 minutes, or until just tender. Do not let the fruit overcook, or it will fall apart and look messy. Keep testing it with a sharp fork as it cooks.

Serving suggestion: Serve warm or cold, with cream or ice cream, if you like.

STRAWBERRY, PEACH, OR BLUEBERRY SHORTCAKE

This is one of the best desserts in the world and not hard to make. You can either make one large shortcake or use individual biscuits.

Serves: 4–6

Preparation time: 30 minutes to mix the biscuit dough, including 15 minutes to preheat oven. You can prepare the fruit while the shortcake is baking. Allow about 15 minutes for preparing fruit.

Cooking time: 15 minutes

What you will need:

1 recipe for biscuit dough (see p. 133) with
   3 extra tablespoons of sugar

3–4 cups strawberries, rinsed, stems cut off,
   and sliced

      or

3 cups peaches, peeled and sliced, with juice
   of ½ lemon squeezed over them to keep
   them from turning brown

      or

3 cups blueberries, rinsed with leaves and
   stems removed

¼ cup sugar

1–2 cups heavy cream, whipped until thick
   but not stiff—so that you can pour it over
   the shortcake

a cookie sheet or round baking pan about
   9 inches across

How to cook it:

For individual shortcakes:

1. Preheat oven to 450°.

2. Roll out dough to ½ inch thickness. Cut out large biscuits, one for each person, 2–3 inches wide with a large glass or cookie cutter or cup. Put them on buttered cookie sheet (½ inch apart) and bake them according to recipe (see

p. 133) . Cool slightly. Split them, either warm or cold. Put fruit inside and a little on top.

3. Sweeten the fruit with 1/4 cup sugar.

4. Whip the cream until it is thick but can still be poured and pour it over each shortcake.

To make one large shortcake:

1. Preheat oven to 425°.

2. Divide the ball of biscuit dough into two parts, one a little bigger than the other. Roll the biggest one out to a circle about 9 inches across and the smaller one out into a slightly small circle, each about 1/2 inch thick. Butter the round cake pan, put the larger circle of dough in it. Lightly spread the top with bits of butter and put the smaller circle on top of it. Bake 12–15 minutes.

3. Sweeten the fruit with 1/4 cup sugar.

4. Whip the cream until it is thick but can still be poured.

5. Separate the shortcakes carefully when slightly cooled and put fruit between the layers and on top. Pour whipped cream over it and serve.

Note: Make sure the sweetened fruit is at room temperature —it will taste much better.

RICH TART PASTRY

Open fruit tarts taste good, look good, and are easier to make than 2-crust pies. This pastry recipe just requires mixing and chilling, but no kneading. It is more or less foolproof. Fill the pastry shell with fresh fruit (see page 162) and bake. Cover it with whipped cream if you like, or pass the cream on the side. You can double the recipe and make two at a time, or even freeze part of it and use later. Just wrap the ball of pastry in foil and store in the freezer. Once you learn how, you will be able to do this very quickly. Butter tastes best in this recipe.

Preparation time: about 1½–2 hours; 20 minutes to make, 40–60 minutes to chill the pastry. Allow 15–20 minutes for preparing the fruit. Do this while the pastry chills.

Cooking time: 25–30 minutes for pie, including 15 minutes to preheat oven

What you will need:

   1 cup flour
   ½ teaspoon salt
   1 tablespoon sugar
   6 tablespoons butter (¾ stick)
   1 egg yolk
   1 tablespoon water
   1½ tablespoons lemon juice

   a flour sifter or sieve

a measuring cup and spoons
2 bowls, 1 good-sized, 1 small
an eggbeater
a rolling pin
a 9-inch pie tin

How to cook it:

1. Put the flour, salt, and sugar into a flour sifter or a good-sized strainer, held over a bowl.

2. Separate the egg (you will not need the white) and put the yolk into a small dish: Have 2 small bowls ready. Then break each egg in half as neatly as you can, holding the egg over one of the bowls. Keep the shell that contains the yolk facing up, so the yolk stays in it. Spill out as much of the white as you can into the bowl under the egg. Then pour the yolk *very gently* back and forth between the two halves of the shell 3 or 4 times, spilling out as much of the white as you can each time. Try not to break it. Finally, put the yolk into the other bowl. Don't worry if there is a little white attached to it, or if it does break. This takes a little practice. If you mess it up, just set the egg aside for scrambled eggs and start again. With an eggbeater, beat the yolk with the water and lemon juice for a minute. Then stir it into the flour in the large bowl. Stir until well mixed, and make it into a ball with your hands. Wrap it in wax paper or a dish towel and put in the refrigerator for 40 minutes.

3. Preheat oven to 425°.

4. When the dough is chilled, sprinkle a little flour on a board or table and on your rolling pin, and roll the dough out to a little less than ¼ inch thick. Lift it up gently and fit it into a 9-inch pie tin. If it tears, just press the torn edges back together. Fill with fruit filling (see pages 162–164) and bake for 25 minutes (check it after 20 minutes).

5. Cool and serve with whipped cream.

Frozen Pie Crust

Nearly every supermarket carries frozen pie crust. It is surprisingly good and very convenient. You can put together a pie in 20 minutes with it. (Remember to defrost the shell for at least 15 minutes before you use it.) Follow the directions on the package for preparing it and fill it with any of the fillings listed following. You may want to use half a cup more fruit and a little more sugar. Pinch the edges together, cut a few slits in the top crust to let the steam out, and bake according to the directions on the package, usually 45 minutes–1 hour. Put the pie tin on a cookie sheet so the fruit will not drip onto the oven.

FRUIT FILLINGS
for Open Tarts or Regular Pies

Preparation time: 20 minutes, including 15 minutes to preheat oven

Cooking time: 25–30 minutes in the pastry shell

Apple Filling

What you will need:

> 6–8 tart apples, depending on size (green
>   apples or Macintosh are good)
> ½–¾ cup sugar
> ½ teaspoon cinnamon
> 1 tablespoon lemon juice
> ¼ teaspoon salt
>
> a medium-sized bowl

How to prepare it:

1. Preheat oven to 425°.

2. Peel and slice the apples fairly thin to make 3 cups.

3. Mix with the sugar, cinnamon, lemon juice, and salt. Arrange in an uncooked tart crust or pie crust (see p. 159, or p. 161 for frozen pie crust).

4. If you are making an open tart, it is sometimes fun to make a pattern of the apple slices, but this is not necessary.

5. Bake 25–30 minutes.

Blueberry Filling

What you will need:

2½ cups blueberries, washed, with leaves and
   stems removed
½ cup sugar
1 tablespoon lemon juice
1 tablespoon flour

a medium-sized bowl

How to prepare it:

1. Preheat oven to 425°.

2. Mix everything together lightly and pile into unbaked pie or tarts shell (see p. 159 or p. 161 for frozen pie crust) .

3. Bake 25 minutes.

Peach or Plum Filling

Peel and slice 2½ cups of fruit and do the same as for blueberry filling.

BEAUTIFUL STRAWBERRY PIE

A glaze is poured over fresh strawberries which makes them shiny and sweet.

Preparation time: 1 hour; make the glaze while the pastry chills

Cooking time: 25 minutes for the pastry

What you will need:

1 recipe rich tart pastry (see p. 159 or p. 161 for frozen pie crust)
2½ cups large ripe strawberries (about 2 pint boxes)
a 9-inch pie tin

For the glaze:

1 cup sugar
3 tablespoons cornstarch
¼ teaspoon salt
1 teaspoon lemon juice

How to prepare it:

1. Boil all the ingredients for the glaze together for ½ hour over low heat.

2. Bake a tart shell according to directions.

3. Wash 2½ cups of strawberries in a strainer or colander and cut the stems off them.

4. Arrange the strawberries, stem end down, in the cooked pie shell. Then pour the syrup over them. Chill the pie for ½ hour in the refrigerator, cover with a layer of whipped cream (see p. 170) , and serve.

Note: This method can be used with any really ripe fruit that is fairly soft, such as cut-up peaches or blueberries.

GINGERBREAD

This is delicious for dessert, served hot with whipped cream. It will keep for several days and is good anytime with a glass of milk or some applesauce. **Note:** this calls for baking SODA, not baking powder.

Preparation time: 20 minutes, including 15 minutes to preheat oven

Cooking time: 30 minutes

What you will need:

   2 eggs
   ½ cup sour cream

½ cup molasses
½ cup brown sugar
1½ cups sifted flour
1 teaspoon baking soda
1 teaspoon powdered ginger
1 teaspoon cinnamon
½ cup melted butter (1 stick)

a sieve or flour sifter
a large bowl for mixing
a small pan for melting butter
a square pan for baking, 8 or 9 inches on each
 side
an eggbeater

How to cook it:

1. Preheat oven to 350°.

2. Melt butter in small pot. Turn off heat as soon as it is melted.

3. Break the eggs into the bowl and beat them well. Add the sour cream, the molasses, and the sugar.

4. Hold the flour sifter over a 2-cup measuring cup and sift flour until you have 1½ cups. Then sift in the baking soda, ginger, and cinnamon. Pour all of these ingredients into the bowl with the eggs and molasses, and stir everything together very well, using a spoon. When no flour at all is showing and there are no more lumps, pour it into the baking pan and bake for 30 minutes.

Serving suggestion: Serve hot, if possible, with whipped cream.

CHOCOLATE MOUSSE

This can be made a day ahead. However, it must be chilled for at least 4 hours before serving. If you make the mousse the day before, just leave it in the refrigerator until you are ready to serve.

Serves: 6

Cooking time: In this case, preparation and cooking are almost the same thing. The mousse takes about 45 minutes to 1 hour to make.

What you will need:

6 squares of semi-sweet chocolate *or* half of a
   12-ounce package of semi-sweet chocolate
   bits
1 tablespoon instant coffee
3 tablespoons butter (do not use margarine)
6 eggs, separated
6 tablespoons sugar
½ cup heavy cream

a double boiler (a pot that fits over another
   one so that water can heat or boil in the
   lower one and only slow heat reaches the
   top one) *or* one pot which you set into a
   frying pan full of water
a large bowl
2 medium-sized bowls
6 small individual bowls *or* 1 serving bowl to
   put the mousse in
an eggbeater

How to cook it:

1. Fill the lower part of the double boiler (or fill the frying
   pan) with an inch or two of water over medium heat.
   Then place the upper pot over the hot water. Put the
   chocolate and the instant coffee into the upper pot. Melt
   them, stirring from time to time. This will take about
   20 minutes. When the chocolate is melted, add the butter
   and melt it with the chocolate.

2. While the chocolate is melting, separate the eggs: break
   them neatly and pour the whites into one of the medium-
   sized bowls. Pour the yolk gently back and forth from one
   half shell to the other a few times, pouring out the white
   from the other shell each time. Put the yolks into the large
   bowl.

3. Beat the egg yolks with the eggbeater for a minute or two,
   until they are a light yellow. Pour the melted chocolate
   mixture into the yolks a little at a time, stirring well with

a spoon as you go, until the yolks and chocolate are well mixed and smooth-looking. Don't pour the chocolate in too fast because the heat might curdle the eggs.

4. Wash the eggbeater and dry it as well as you can (it's not easy). Beat the egg whites until they stand up in stiff peaks.

5. Wipe the egg whites off the beater with a paper towel and whip the cream in the other medium-sized bowl until it is stiff. Beat in the sugar at the end.

6. Very gently, fold the egg whites into the chocolate–egg mixture, and then fold in the whipped cream. Use a large metal or wooden spoon or a rubber spatula. Move it down through the mixture on the side farthest from you, then keep moving it toward you along the bottom of the dish, and bring it up on the side near you. Keep repeating until ingredients are fairly well mixed. Folding is a way of gently mixing beaten egg whites or whipped cream with another ingredient so that the air stays in them. As you will see, it is a folding motion, bringing the heavier ingredient up from the bottom and tucking the lighter one down into it. It does not mix things as thoroughly as stirring, but that does not matter here. Try to keep the mixture as fluffy as you can, but do make sure that no white patches show when it is all mixed.

7. Pour into 1 large bowl or 6 small bowls and chill in the refrigerator for at least 4 hours.

Serving suggestion: Serve plain or with whipped cream.

WHIPPED CREAM

For one 9-inch pie, use 1 small container (½ pint) *heavy* cream. It is the only kind thick enough to be whipped. It will whip better if it is chilled. Pour it into any deep container, such as a large measuring cup or small deep bowl. Beat with an eggbeater or an electric mixer until it is thick. Or you can whirl it in a blender for a minute or two. Be careful not to whip it too long or it will begin to turn into butter. If you like, add 1 tablespoon sugar and ½ teaspoon vanilla. Keep it cold until ready to use.

CINNAMON TOAST

Serves: 4

Preparation time: 5 minutes

What you will need:

8 slices white bread (2 for each person)
4 tablespoons sugar
2½ teaspoons cinnamon
4 tablespoons butter (½ stick)

How to cook it:

1. Toast the bread.

2. Mix the sugar and cinnamon while the bread is toasting.

3. Butter the bread generously.

4. Sprinkle with plenty of the sugar and cinnamon mixture.

5. Cut slices in half and serve immediately.

FRENCH TOAST

If you have some bread that is a little old or hard, this is a good way to use it. Otherwise, use slices of fresh bread.

Serves: 4

Preparation time: 5 minutes

Cooking time: 15 minutes

What you will need:

8 slices bread, stale or fresh
1½ cups milk
3 eggs
1 teaspoon cinnamon
2 tablespoons sugar

a bowl large enough to soak the bread in, 3
    slices at a time
a heavy frying pan or griddle

How to cook it:

1. Grease the frying pan or griddle with a little oil, butter,
   or margarine, and put it over medium heat while you prepare the bread.

2. Pour the milk into the bowl; break in the eggs, and add
   the cinnamon and sugar. With a fork or eggbeater, beat
   everything together until well mixed. Dip the bread slices,
   3 at a time, into the egg and milk, let them soak for a minute, and put them into the hot frying pan. When they are
   brown on one side (about 5 minutes), turn them and
   brown on the other side. They will take about 10–15 minutes to do.

Serving suggestions: Serve when they are well-browned, with jam, honey, or maple syrup.

HOBO EGGS

This is a very satisfying variation on a fried egg.

Preparation time: none

Cooking time: 5–10 minutes

What you will need:

eggs (1 per person)
1 slice of bread for each egg
½–1 stick butter or margarine

a small cookie cutter or very small glass
a heavy frying pan
a spatula

How to cook them:

1. Melt the butter or margarine in the frying pan. Begin with ½ stick for 2 slices of bread and 2 eggs, and add more as you need it.

2. With the cookie cutter or glass, cut circles of bread out of

the middle of each slice of bread, and put the punched-out slices of bread into the pan to brown. (You can put the circles in the pan to brown, too, if you like.) After about 3 minutes, when the bread is golden brown on one side, turn the slices over and break an egg into the hole in each slice. The hole will hold the yolk and the white will spread over the bread. Don't worry if it's a little messy. Let it cook for 2 minutes and spoon melted butter or margarine over the top. Then turn it over with a quick flip of your wrist and cook for 2 more minutes on the other side. If you are not good at flipping, add more butter to the pan, and keep spooning hot melted butter over the yolk and white of each egg until it is well-cooked. You should be able to do 2 hobo eggs at a time in an average-sized frying pan.

Serving suggestion: Serve the browned circles of bread on the side if you have cooked them. Serve with bacon or home-fried potatoes which you have cooked ahead.

MARIAN'S COFFEECAKE

This takes less than an hour from start to finish, and if you get up a little early on Sunday morning it can be a breakfast surprise for your family. It's good in the afternoon, too, with milk or tea.

Preparation time: 20–30 minutes, including 15 minutes to preheat oven.

Cooking time: 30 minutes

What you will need:

½ stick butter or margarine
⅓ cup sugar
1 egg
⅔ cup milk
1½ cups flour
2 teaspoons baking powder
½ teaspoon salt
½ teaspoon vanilla
sieve or flour sifter

a 9-inch cake pan, round or square (8-inch will
    do, too)
a bowl for mixing

For the topping:

2 tablespoons sugar
1½ teaspoons cinnamon
1–2 tablespoons butter

Add if you like:

1 small apple, quartered, peeled, cored and
    very thinly sliced

How to cook it:

1. Put the butter into the bowl on top of the stove to soften for 10 or 15 minutes. Do not let it melt.

2. Preheat oven to 375°.

3. Grease the baking pan with butter or margarine.

4. Beat the butter in the bowl with a wooden spoon until it is soft (about 5 minutes) and stir in the sugar. Beat them well together for 2 or 3 minutes, until the mixture is smooth. Add the egg and the milk and stir again for a minute.

5. Measure the flour into a 2-cup measuring cup, and add the baking powder and salt. Hold the sieve or sifter over the bowl with the butter mixture, and pour the flour, baking powder and salt into the sifter. Sift it into the butter; then add the vanilla and stir everything together until no flour shows and the mixture looks smooth.

6. Pour the mixture into the greased baking pan.

7. Mix 2 tablespoons sugar with 1½ teaspoons cinnamon, and sprinkle it on top of the batter. Put 5 or 6 small bits of butter around on top of that, and bake for 30 minutes.

Note: For an apple topping, arrange one very thinly sliced apple on top of the coffeecake (make some sort of pattern if you want with the slices). Sprinkle the sugar and cinnamon mixture on top of it, and put the bits of butter on and bake according to above instructions.

PANCAKES

Serves: 4

Preparation time: 15 minutes

Cooking time: 10–15 minutes

What you will need:

1 cup sifted flour
2 teaspoons baking powder
1 tablespoon sugar
½ teaspoon salt
½ cup milk
2 tablespoons cooking oil
1 egg

a flour sifter or sieve
a bowl for mixing
a heavy frying pan or griddle

How to cook it:

1. Rub a tablespoon of cooking oil over the frying pan or griddle and put it over low heat while you are mixing the batter. The pan must be very hot when you are ready to cook the pancakes.

2. Sift flour into a measuring cup until it measures 1 cup. Then add the baking powder, sugar, and salt. Sift them all together into the mixing bowl. Add the milk, the egg, and

the cooking oil, and stir with a fork until smoothly mixed and no flour shows. Turn the heat up to medium-high.

3. The batter should be just thin enough so that it pours easily from a spoon or ladle, like heavy cream. Add more milk (a little) if you need to. Pour 3 or 4 small to medium-sized pancakes onto the frying pan or griddle with a spoon or ladle. When there are small bubbles all over each one and the edges swell a little, turn them with a spatula and brown them on the other side. They should be golden brown on both sides. Turning them takes a little practice, but it is not hard. If the first few don't turn out, discard them and start again.

Serving suggestions: Serve with jam, honey, or maple syrup.

Apple Pancakes

To the batter for pancakes, above, add one apple, quartered, peeled, cored, and thinly sliced. Cook as above.

Blueberry Pancakes

To the batter for pancakes, above, add one cup of blueberries, washed and with stems and leaves removed. Cook as above.

Thin Pancakes with Jam

To the batter for pancakes, above, add 1 more tablespoon sugar and ¼ cup milk. Cook as above. (They will spread out more, because the batter is thinner.) Put a spoonful or two of good jam in each one and roll it up. Spread a little butter over the top and serve. This can be a dessert as well as a breakfast.

Suggested Menus

SOME SPECIAL BREAKFASTS

Fresh orange juice
Peach shortcake, served warm
    with unsweetened whipped cream
Milk or hot chocolate or coffee or tea

Grapefruit halves
Apple or blueberry pancakes
    with maple syrup, honey, or jam
Breakfast sausages
Milk or hot chocolate or coffee or tea

Fresh strawberries to dip in sugar
Marian's coffeecake
Milk or hot chocolate or coffee or tea

Fresh orange juice
Fried ham and eggs and home-fried potatoes
Hot biscuits
Milk or hot chocolate or coffee or tea

Fresh fruit bowl
French toast with maple syrup,
    honey, or jam
Bacon
Milk or hot chocolate or coffee or tea

SOME SPECIAL WEEKEND OR HOLIDAY LUNCHES

(These could also be light suppers after large dinners)

Split pea soup with frankfurters
Hot cornbread and butter
Baked apples with cream

Cold sliced ham
Bean salad and hot biscuits
Apple brown Betty

Vegetable soup with parmesan cheese
Roast beef sandwiches with mustard
   and dill pickles on pumpernickel
   on rye bread
Warm blueberry cake

Black bean soup
Chef's salad
Applesauce and Carolyn's ginger cookies

Cold meat loaf sandwiches
Cole slaw
Fresh fruit and brownies

SOME DINNER MENUS

A week-night dinner for 4 or 5 that is easy to prepare:

Irish lamb stew
Green salad
Apple brown Betty

A company dinner for 6 that is easy to prepare:

Roast leg of lamb with mustard
Boiled new potatoes with butter and parsley
Cold green bean salad
Chocolate mousse

A buffet dinner for 8–10 people:

Baked lasagne
Green salad
Open apple tarts with whipped cream

Another informal buffet dinner for 8–10 people:

Black beans
Picadillo
Rice
Cooked sliced bananas
Green salad
Raspberry sherbet with butter cookies with jam centers

*Two week-night dinners for 6 that you can
mostly prepare the day before:*

Pot roast
Egg noodles
Green salad
Cooked fruit in syrup

Boiled beef with vegetables
Blueberry tart with cream

A company meal for 6 people in spring:

Roast chickens with pan-roasted potatoes and carrots
Cold asparagus with French dressing
Beautiful strawberry pie

A good quick dinner for 4 people:

Leftover meat with rice, scallions, and soy sauce
Sliced tomato salad
Fresh fruit with Carolyn's ginger cookies

Two simple meals for 4–6 people:

Broiled marinated flank steak
Corn on the cob
Green salad
Warm gingerbread with whipped cream

Meat loaf
Baked potatoes
Green salad
Apple pie

A company dinner for 6:

Cold artichokes with French dressing
Roast beef with pan-roasted potatoes
Green salad
Chocolate mousse

Index

HB7G